# THE TAO OF
# *AppleScript*

# Other BMUG Publications

### *The BMUG Newsletter*
Semi-annual Membership benefit

### *Zen and the Art of Resource Editing*
### *The BMUG Guide to ResEdit, Third Edition*
by Derrick Schneider, Hans Hansen, Noah Potkin

### *BMUG's Quicker QuickTime*
by Judi Stern & Robert Lettieri

### *The 1993 BMUG Shareware Disk Catalog*

### *The BMUG Guide to Bulletin Boards and Beyond*
by Bernard Aboba

### *The Beginner's ResEdit*
Zen and the Art of Resource Editing, Japanese translation

# THE TAO OF
# *AppleScript*

by Derrick Schneider
edited by Tim Holmes

**BMUG**

Library of Congress Catalog No.: 93-79095
ISBN: 1-56830-075-1

95   94                    4   3

Interpretation of the printing code: the rightmost double-digit number is the year of the book's printing; the rightmost single-digit number the number of the book's printing. For example, a printing code of 93-1 shows that the first printing of the book occurred in 1993.

Trademark Acknowledgments: All products mentioned in this book are either trademarks of the companies referenced in this book, registered trademarks of the companies referenced in this book, or neither. We strongly advise that you investigate a particular product's name thoroughly before you use the name as your own. Apple, Mac, and Macintosh are all registered trademarks of Apple Computer, Inc.

# *Limits of liability and disclaimer of warranty*

BMUG's licensor(s) makes no warranties, express or implied, including without limitation the implied warranties of merchantability and fitness for a particular purpose, regarding the software. BMUG's licensor(s) does not warrant, guarantee or make any representations regarding the use or the results of the use of the software in terms of its correctness, accuracy, reliability, currentness or otherwise. The entire risk as the results and performance of the software is assumed by you. The exclusion of implied warranties is not permitted by some jurisdictions. The above exclusion may not apply to you.

In no event will BMUG's licensor(s), and their directors, officers, employees or agents (collectively BMUG's licensor) be liable to you for any consequential, incidental or indirect damages (including damages for loss of business profits, business interruption, loss of business information, and the life) arising out of the use or inability to use the software even if BMUG's licensor has been advised of the possibility of such damages. Because some jurisdictions do not allow the exclusion or limitation of liability for consequential or incidental damages, the above limitations may not apply to you. BMUG's licensor's liability to you for actual damages from any cause whatsoever, and regardless of the form of the action (whether in contract, tort (including negligence), product liability or otherwise), will be limited to $50.

Design and Editing
**Hans Hansen**

Project Coordinator
**Kelly Pernell**

Additional Editing
**Gary Shaw**
**Chris Holmes**

Additional Review
**Raines Cohen**
**Mario Murphy**

Software Contributions
**Greg Dow**
**Chris Reed**
**Joe Zobkiw**

Hayden Production Staff
**Diana Bigham, Katy Bodenmiller, Scott Cook,
Tim Cox, Meshell Dinn, Mark Enochs,
Tom Loveman, Roger Morgan, Beth Rago,
Carrie Roth, Greg Simsic, Kevin Spear**

Composed in stone serif, stone sans serif and
stone informal.

# Dedication

*This book is dedicated to BMUG.*

*Individuals that helped me to grow and*
*gave me experiences I never would have had.*

*—Derrick Schneider*

# Acknowledgments

While our attitude and our goals are an important part of this book, there's a great deal more to it. This book would not have been possible without help from the following people.

Mark Thomas, Apple's AppleScript Evangelist, who helped us become a seed site for AppleScript, and was willing to answer any questions we tossed his way.

The AppleScript team, who not only made some way cool software, but were willing to answer questions when Mark couldn't.

Carol Espinosa, the current AppleScript Evangelist, who went out of her way to help us when we needed it and got us the very latest software so this book could be as accurate as possible.

Lastly, BMUG and David Rogelberg for putting our dreams to paper.

## About BMUG

BMUG is a membership-based non-profit organization dedicated to helping users of graphical interface computers. It represents the interests of over 12,000 Macintosh users in more than fifty countries.

BMUG started as a small user group in 1984, shortly after the introduction of the Macintosh. As a non-profit corporation BMUG strives to give the plain, unbiased truths about product performance and the industry in general. We don't sell advertising in our newsletters and make it quite clear that we will not exchange good reviews for product donations. BMUG is neither affiliated with, nor receives monetary support from Apple Computer or any other for-profit entity.

## We Want to Hear from You

What our readers think of Hayden Books is crucial to our sense of well-being. If you have any comments, no matter how great or how small, we'd appreciate your taking the time to send us a note.

David Rogelberg
Hayden Books
11711 N. College Ave.
Carmel, IN 46032
(800) 428-5331 voice
(800) 448-3804 fax

# *Foreword*

What's the best part of your Mac? The mouse? The icons? The menus? Alas, but these very niceties sometimes get in your way.

Ever want to automatically move folders around? Or program your Mac to search out all your big files? Maybe you need to filter fifty chapters of a book through a spell checker, a formatter, and then into PageMaker?

Sure, you could do all these with your mouse and menus. But you'd go nuts moving all these around. Wouldn't it be nifty to have a single command that moves those folders around for you? How about writing your own program to slide those fifty chapters into the word processor?

Aaah: That's why you need AppleScript. It's a language that lets you mechanize these routine operations. Lets your mind work on the creative, and saves wear on your mouse.

It's a simple language with commands like "tell", "make", "create", and "quit". AppleScript automates the mundane and gives you control of your computer. Saving time for users.

Like BMUG: a group dedicated to saving time and troubles for Macintosh users around the world. No surprise that the good people of BMUG have written the first book about a language that brings script programming to your Mac.

From the back alleys of Berkeley, where you'll find apple cores and well groomed mice, comes this guide to AppleScript. It won't replace the best part of your Mac; it'll make it better.

— Cliff Stoll

# Table of Contents at a Glance

# *The Tao of AppleScript*

───────────── ☯ ─────────────

# *Preface*

## The Tao of Who?

During the making of this book, many titles were tossed around. Among these, *The Tao of AppleScript* quickly became our favorite. In some ways, this title suggested itself. It may seem like just a cute, gimmicky title for a book about scripting, but we feel it embodies the spirit and purpose of this book.

*Zen and the Art of Resource Editing,* a BMUG book created in part by Derrick and Hans, incorporated the philosophy of Zen Buddhism into its approach to teaching. Our approach to AppleScript incorporates the underlying principles of Taoism into the way this book conveys its meaning and teaches its subject. Another play on a popular book title that includes a reference to an Eastern religion, *The Tao of Pooh,* seemed appropriate.

Taoism is markedly different from other Eastern religions. While many of them are heavily laden with ritual, Taoism is marked by a decided lack of specific rites to perform. Simplicity is the primary focus, and this is also how AppleScript was designed—to be simple and flexible. Its power is in its lack of structure. It cannot be approached by learning to obey a rigid set of rules. For this reason it made sense to abandon the traditional textbook approach.

Because of the historical differences between Western and Eastern written languages, there is no way to phonetically spell "Tao" the way it is pronounced in Chinese. The closest, most common pronunciation is "dow" as in "Dow Jones."

When creating the *Zen* book, we set out to show people that ResEdit, a tool normally reserved for power users, could be used by beginners just as easily. What's more, we wanted to show people how much fun it could be. People read the book and said, "Wow, this *really* is cool," and proceeded to try things they never would have dared to before.

That kind of response feels good. It means that people didn't simply learn to use ResEdit; they learned how to do things we never taught them, to explore on their own.

That's what we hope to accomplish with *The Tao of AppleScript.* Not simply to teach you to use AppleScript, but to inspire you. We want you to feel the same way about AppleScript that we do—obsessed!

Taoism's followers are encouraged to explore and discover their own paths to realization and awareness, and so too we encourage you to find your own path to using AppleScript. As you read, we encourage you to take time to play with AppleScript. Write scripts, even simple ones. Take breaks and come back to the book after you've explored a bit.

Just as each must find his own Way in Taoism, so must one find his own Way in AppleScript.

# *Introduction*
## The Way of AppleScript

Imagine being able to set up complex, time-consuming, and tedious tasks and then sit back and watch your Macintosh perform them flawlessly. Better yet, imagine automating tasks that may have taken days or even weeks to do manually—running them overnight while sitting at home enjoying a good book, and returning in the morning to find the task complete.

Imagine being able to add your own features to an application that doesn't do everything you want, or perhaps has features that aren't quite right. Or maybe an application doesn't exist to do what you need.

Imagine being able to create a program to fit your needs and suit your tastes without going through the headache of learning a traditional programming language. Or for that matter, imagine being able to program and have fun doing it.

All these things are a reality with AppleScript. These are the things that make AppleScript great. You *can* make your Mac do the things that you want. It's so easy—you can even enjoy doing it.

## What is it?

AppleScript is a scripting language. Scripting languages have all the capabilities of other programming languages, but are easier to use. Scripts can store data for later use, and evaluate their surroundings to decide what to do next. They also can loop through certain instructions, repeating them as many times as you like, or until something you specify happens. These features, and others, are what make a scripting language—particularly AppleScript— ideal for anyone who wants to automate a task.

Many applications have incorporated their own scripting language for automating tasks. The best known example is HyperCard, which includes a full scripting language for manipulating every aspect of its interface. Other applications with scripting capabilities include: FileMaker, PageMaker, Excel, MicroPhone, and WordPerfect.

AppleScript differs because its control isn't limited to a single application. AppleScript is a part of the Macintosh Operating System, and this enables it to work with many different applications at once, even on several Macs across a network. It can control and gather information from those applications and then direct others to process that data. It not only automates tasks, but can control the flow of information from one application to another.

As an example of what scripting can do, look at the first edition of BMUG's disk catalog. This 700-page book lists our entire Shareware library with a description, author information, icon, size and compatibility listing for each of its 3,600 files, drawn from twenty-two FileMaker Pro databases. The process of manually bringing that information into PageMaker for layout was a huge and time-consuming task. Not only was it inherently difficult to deal with the sheer volume of information, the format of the book specified fifteen chapters with six different layouts.

All these factors took an enormous amount of time: ten months to plan and produce the entire book, including four months of manual layout work. For the subsequent edition, there simply wasn't that kind of time. To facilitate the production process, a scripting language (UserLand Frontier, a language functionally similar to AppleScript) was used to automate the entire production. The script passed through each database and then moved the data of each record to the page layout program, formatting it and positioning it as it was brought in. The entire development time for the scripts was six weeks and the scripts ran for ten days laying out the book.

While that's an extreme example of what can be done, it gives you an idea of the power of a scripting language. You can use AppleScript to do very basic things as well, such as emptying the trash every hour or whenever.

This book will show you how to take advantage of the power of AppleScript. It also will show you the mechanics of the language itself and will teach you how to develop your own scripts from scratch, helping you through each step of the scripting process.

By the time you've read through this book, you'll understand how to fully exploit AppleScript. You may even realize that AppleScript is not only useful—it can quickly become an obsession.

# *The Journey Begins*

To use AppleScript, you must first install it on your Macintosh. You need System 7.1 or, if you are using System 7.0 or 7.0.1, you will also need QuickTime 1.5 or later.

System 7.0 + QuickTime

On the disk included with this book you'll find the files you need for AppleScript. They are compressed into a StuffIt document. To uncompress this document, double-click on the item named *Tao Installer*. This brings up a save dialog box. Click Save and the document uncompresses into a folder called Tao Disk Stuff on the top or "root" level of your hard drive. You will need about two and a half megabytes of free space on your hard drive for the software on the disk.

Tao Installer

Within the folder Tao Disk Stuff, you will find two folders. The first folder, Install These…, includes files that need to be put in specific places on your hard drive: AppleScript™, Apple® Event Manager, QuickTime™ (within a folder called "System 7.0(.1) users only"), and a folder entitled Scripting Additions.

Install These…

Apple® Event Manager

AppleScript™

Scripting Additions

Tao AppleScript

The first two items, Apple Event Manager and AppleScript, can be dropped onto the System Folder of your hard drive and will automatically be placed in the Extensions folder. If you are using System 7.0 or 7.0.1, QuickTime must also be placed in your Extensions folder.

The Scripting Additions folder must be manually placed in the Extensions folder by opening your System Folder and dropping it onto your Extensions folder.

The second folder, Tao AppleScript, includes: the applications Script Editor, Scriptable Text Editor, Progress Bar, Finder Liaison, and StuffIt Lite, all of which can be placed anywhere on your hard drive; the scripting additions ResMover, and DialogRunner, which need to be placed in the Scripting Additions folder; and Folder Watcher, a combination control panel and extension, which can be dropped onto your System Folder. The control panel and extension will be automatically placed in their respective folders.

After placing these files in their appropriate folders, restart your computer to enable the system to use the AppleScript extensions.

## What did you Install?

The AppleScript extension is the core of AppleScript. It includes the language that enables AppleScript to talk to applications and control their actions.

The term "AppleScript aware" describes an application that can be controlled by AppleScript. The term "AppleScript recordable" describes an application that reports the user's actions within that application to the System; AppleScript can then record those actions and turn them into a script.

The Apple Event Manager gives AppleScript the capability to record your actions. Applications that are AppleScript-aware *and* recordable allow AppleScript to watch what you do and automatically turn your actions into a script. This is similar to a macro utility; however, you can fully edit the resulting scripts. Apple Event Manager, like the AppleScript extension itself, is required to run AppleScript and write scripts.

QuickTime is only necessary if you are *not* running System 7.1. This is because System 7.1 has the "component manager" portion of QuickTime integrated, while Systems 7.0 and 7.0.1 do not. This component manager is necessary for AppleScript to operate.

The Scripting Additions folder contains files called scripting additions that extend the language of AppleScript. An example of this is Beep, an addition that gives AppleScript the capability to beep. Included with this book are the scripting additions that Apple bundles with AppleScript: Beep, Choose Application, Choose File, Current Date, Display Dialog, File Commands, Load Script, Numerics, Run Script, Store Script, and String Commands. In addition, the Tao AppleScript folder contains a couple of scripting additions written especially for this book: ResMover and DialogRunner.

Script Editor is the application you will use to write, edit, compile, and run scripts.

Scriptable Text Editor is completely AppleScript aware and recordable. As a word processor, it's fairly simple, but since it is "AppleScript-aware," it is used throughout this book in example scripts.

Also in the Tao AppleScript folder you will find: Progress Bar, which allows your scripts to show a status indicator revealing their progress; Finder Liaison, an application that allows a bit of control over the Finder's functions; and StuffIt Lite, a popular Shareware compression program by Aladdin Systems that supports AppleScript.

Finally, FolderWatcher, an AppleScript-aware control panel, enables AppleScript to watch certain folders for a specified activity and run a script when that activity occurs.

## First Look at Script Editor

Now that the software is installed, you should launch Script Editor and take a look at it. When you first open Script Editor, you'll see a window with three buttons that work like the buttons on a tape recorder (see figure 1.1). The Stop button interrupts the script currently running (typing Command-period achieves the same effect). The Record button (Command-D) tells AppleScript to

**Note:** You should install all of this software before reading on so that you can follow the text.

record your actions in a recordable application and write them as a script in the script editing area. The Run button (Command-R) runs the script.

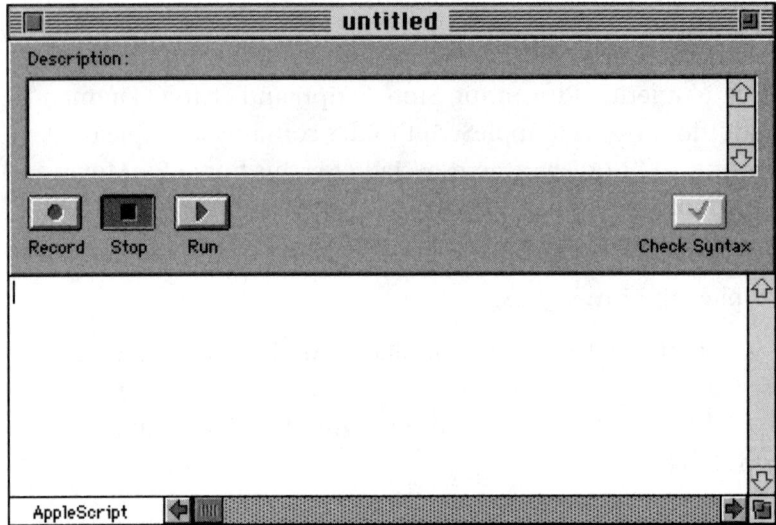

**Figure 1.1**
*Script Editor when
it is first opened.*

The field at the top of the window is for comments about that script. This can be a useful place for a summary of the script's function. The field at the bottom is where you will type in and edit scripts, and view recorded scripts.

## The Littlest Script

As you read on, you will become more familiar with the parts of the window. You can begin now by writing a simple script. In the script editing area, type the following:

```
3+3
```

As you enter this text, the rightmost button in the control area, Check Syntax, will become active (see figure 1.2). Clicking this button checks your script for syntax errors and formats the text to make it easier to read. This process is called "compiling." You can click the Check Syntax button (or press the Enter key) to format the simple script you just entered. It will look like this:

---

3 + 3

---

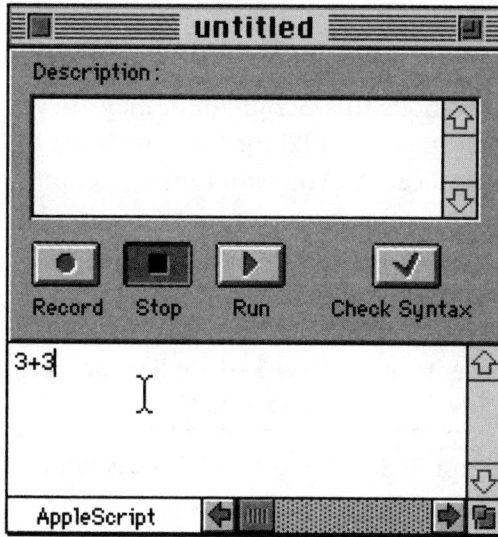

*Figure 1.2*
*Typing in a script.*

While you probably didn't notice much difference, AppleScript did format the text. Notice that the font changed and spaces were added between the 3s and the plus symbol.

Once you've compiled a script by clicking on the Check Syntax button, you can then run it by clicking the Run button (or by pressing Command-R). For a shortcut, you don't need to check the syntax of a script if you are about to run it anyway. Running a script automatically compiles the script first.

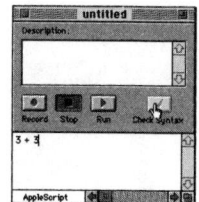

When you run this script, a window entitled "the result" will appear. Script Editor places the last piece of information the script obtained—the result—into this window. Since this script gets the result of 3 + 3, the result window contains the number 6.

After clicking Check Syntax and compiling the script.

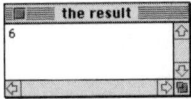

The result of this particular script is 6.

## Using Other Programs

One of the key features of AppleScript is its capability to control and communicate with many applications. To see how this works, type this text in the script editing area:

> set the contents of window 1 of application "Scriptable Text Editor" to "My first AppleScript script."

When you compile this, Script Editor may ask you to find the application Scriptable Text Editor. Use the dialog box that appears to locate the application. You won't need to point to Scriptable Text Editor again, unless you move it to another location or change its name, as AppleScript remembers its location. The compiled script will look like this:

> **set the contents of window 1 of application** "Scriptable Text Editor" *to* "My first AppleScript script."

Run this script. If Scriptable Text Editor is not currently running, AppleScript will start it. The script will place the phrase "My first AppleScript script" into the first window (that is, the frontmost window) of that application (see figure 1.3).

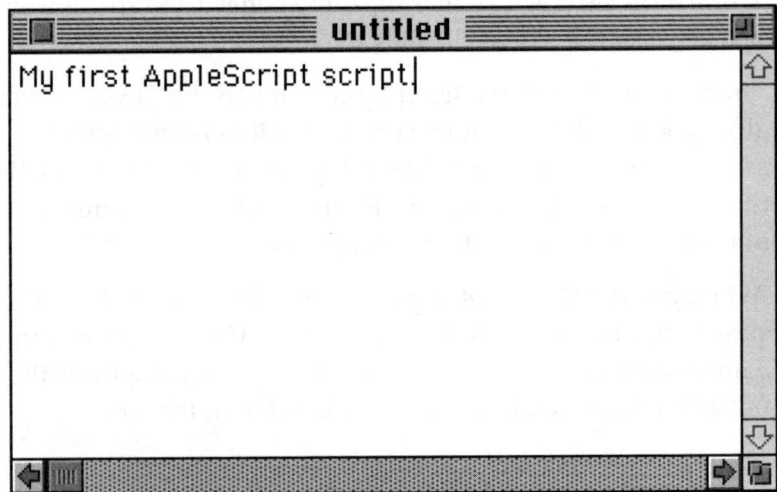

***Figure 1.3***
*The results of your first AppleScript script!*

You have just seen how AppleScript can control other applications.

## Dictionaries

Now that you have a basic understanding of the scripting area of Script Editor, there are a few menu items you should know about.

As with most Macintosh applications, Script Editor enables you to create new documents and open or close a document from the File menu. In addition, Script Editor gives you the capability to open the "dictionary" of an application.

When AppleScript first addresses an application, it knows nothing about what that program can or cannot do. It asks the program for a list of commands it can accept and information that it can manipulate. This dictionary is stored within the application. Using the Open Dictionary command in the File menu enables you to take a look at one of these lists for yourself. Try Scriptable Text Editor's dictionary (see figure 1.4).

Clicking on a specific word in the left side of the dictionary window shows you information about that word. As you write the scripts in this book, the commands you need will be provided for you. When you are writing scripts on your own, or exploring the vocabulary of new programs, you'll find the dictionaries an invaluable resource.

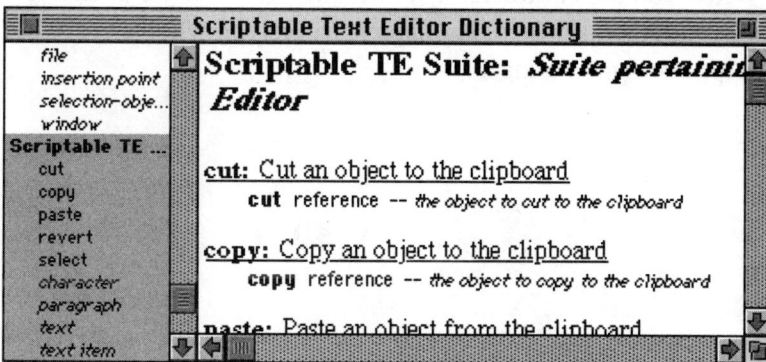

**Figure 1.4**
*Scriptable Text Editor's dictionary.*

## Formatting

AppleScript, as you have seen, formats the text with styles and fonts so that a script is easier to read. To see the formatting rules it follows, choose the AppleScript Formatting command in the Edit menu. If you want to change the way AppleScript formats text in the script editing area, select a category in the AppleScript Formatting dialog box and choose a font, size, or style from the menu bar. The default settings will be used for the examples in this book, so you may want to leave them in order to follow along more easily until you become more familiar with scripting.

## Saving

In addition to being able to save a script as a standard format script file, Script Editor enables you to save a script as "run-only." This is a script that runs and performs its function, but cannot be edited.

You'll recognize most of the other commands in Script Editor, since they're common to most Macintosh programs.

## On Your Own

Becoming familiar with Script Editor's landscape is the first step of your journey. Feel free to look around and play with the parts you've seen so far. Try scripts based upon those we've given you.

When you are comfortable (or bored) with how Script Editor works, move on to the next chapter, where you will learn about the AppleScript language.

# The Threshold of Adventure

You've seen how AppleScript can perform simple tasks, such as placing text into a window or adding numbers together. It can, of course, do much more. The AppleScript language provides the tools necessary for virtually any scripting task.

There are five main parts to AppleScript: *objects*, which point to items and information within applications; *commands*, which act on those items or information; *variables*, which enable you to store data for later use; *conditionals*, which enable your script to make decisions based on sets of conditions; and *repeat loops*, which give the capability to execute commands repeatedly.

## Objects

The most important aspect of AppleScript is that it can work with data from many applications. Each item or piece of information that AppleScript deals with is considered an object.

Each AppleScript-aware application contains a list of the objects it uses and how AppleScript can manipulate them. Without this list AppleScript would not know what the application is capable of. To help create a standard structure, Apple created the Object

Model—a convention developers are encouraged to follow. Scriptable Text Editor follows this standard.

Take a look at how to address objects. Assume you're interested in the second word in the window shown in figure 2.1.

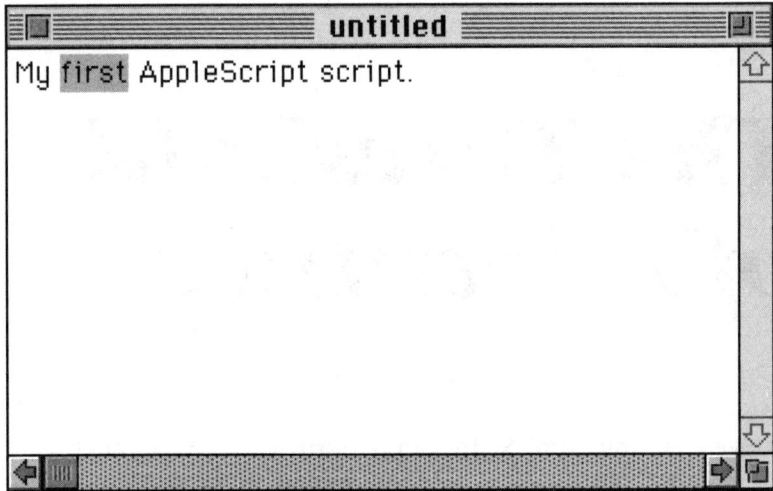

**Figure 2.1**
*The second word in a window of Scriptable Text Editor*

You must specify the type of object you're interested in. Objects generally have names representative of what you may call them everyday. Appropriately enough, the name of this particular type of object is "word."

There are, however, several words present in the window. How can AppleScript know which word you mean? In this case, you want the second word, so the more specific description of this object is "word 2."

Looking at the figure, you see that the second word is found within a "document" or "window" object (these terms are synonymous in Scriptable Text Editor). But there may be more than one window open in your application, so you must tell AppleScript in which window "word 2" is located, just as you had to specify "word 2" to distinguish it from the other words. As with words, you can specify a window using numbers. Windows are numbered from front to back, so the frontmost window will always be "window 1." You can also specify a window by its name, such as "window 'untitled'."

Of course, there may be windows open in more than one application as well. Just as you had to tell AppleScript "word 2 in window 1," you need to tell it which application that particular "window 1" is located in. For this, you specify the "application" object—identifying this application from all others available. You must specify application objects by their name. In this instance, you would write "application 'Scriptable Text Editor'" to indicate the particular application.

The full description (or "object path," in technical parlance) of this object is "word 2 of window 1 of application 'Scriptable Text Editor'." This description is the position of the object relative to others of its kind and relative to its "container" objects. For each step along the path, you must describe each object.

## Properties

In addition to describing objects, you can describe the attributes, or "properties," of that object. You may want to know the font of a particular word. AppleScript allows you to point to these properties, as in "the font of word 2 of window 1 of application 'Scriptable Text Editor'."

## Commands

You need to know the commands to use for controlling the objects you've just learned to describe. Commands act on objects. For instance, when you set the contents of the first window of Scriptable Text Editor, "set" is the command and the contents of the first window is the object.

AppleScript has three types of commands. All three types follow the same rules, but differ in their origins. The first type is built into AppleScript itself, the second type is made up of commands obtained from applications, and the third type is made up of commands from scripting additions.

Here are some examples of each type:

## Set (built-in)

The "set" command assigns the value of an object. When you want to set the value of an object, you must first specify the object you are setting and then specify what the object's value will become, using "to." For instance, in figure 2.1, "the contents of the window of application Scriptable Text Editor" has been set to "The Tao of AppleScript."

---

set the contents of window 1 of application "Scriptable Text Editor" to "The Tao of AppleScript"

---

## Make (from an application)

The "make" command is used to create a new object. For instance, telling Scriptable Text Editor to "make" a window is equivalent to choosing "New" from the File menu.

To make something, you must let AppleScript know what object you want to be made, such as:

---

make window of application "Scriptable Text Editor"

---

AppleScript alone does not understand the "make" command. It is one of the commands that comes from an application. Because Scriptable Text Editor has the "make" command in its dictionary, AppleScript can use it when talking to that application. In fact, if you were to type in and run this script, you would get an error. This is because AppleScript cannot execute the "make" command until it knows that it exists, and it doesn't know it exists until you specify that you are addressing the Scriptable Text Editor application—which isn't done until *after* the command (AppleScript reads from left to right). You will learn how to avoid this problem later.

Many commands, such as set, have required parameters that define the command. For instance, when using the make command, the parameter that defines what to make (and where to make it) is required.

## Beep (from an addition)

The beep command tells your Macintosh to play the sound chosen in the Sound control panel. Here it is:

```
beep
```

You can beep any number of times. To beep twice you would write the following:

```
beep 2
```

The number of beeps is an optional parameter. Commands can work with or without these parameters—that's why they are called optional. If you do supply one, however, it changes the behavior of the command to which it was applied.

The beep command comes from a scripting addition, called Beep, located in the Scripting Additions folder of your Extensions folder. As long as these additions are present, the commands will be available.

As you can see with Beep, scripting additions don't always need to act on objects to function.

Scripting additions are an easy way to add functions to the AppleScript language as you need them.

## Other methods of pointing to objects

As you become more adept with these commands, you'll want more powerful and flexible ways of describing objects. For instance, you may want to work with *all* the objects in a certain window, or a particular subset of those objects.

As an example, by using the "delete" command from Scriptable Text Editor, you could remove specific objects that you describe. You could work with the first three words in a particular window, such as:

```
delete words 1 through 3 of window 1 of application
"Scriptable Text Editor"
```

You can refer to objects by their positions relative to other objects, as in:

---

delete **the** word **before** word 2 **of** window 1 **of** application "Scriptable Text Editor"

delete **the** word **after** word 2 **of** window 1 **of** application "Scriptable Text Editor"

delete **the middle** word **of** window 1 **of** application "Scriptable Text Editor"

---

Sometimes, you may just want *any* object. "Some" points to a random object in a range of objects:

---

delete **some** word **of** window 1 **of** application "Scriptable Text Editor"

---

You may also want to work with every object of a given type. AppleScript provides "every" for this purpose:

---

delete **every** word **of** window 1 **of** application "Scriptable Text Editor"

---

To describe only those objects that meet certain criteria, AppleScript provides the filters "whose" and "where":

The filters "whose" and "where" function identically. Use whichever word reads more naturally.

---

delete (**every** word **of** window 1 **of** application "Scriptable Text Editor" **where** character 1 **is** "f")

delete (**every** word **of** window 1 **of** application "Scriptable Text Editor" **whose** character 1 **is** "f")

---

The many different pointing methods provided by AppleScript give you a lot of flexibility, which enables you to use commands efficiently. You can do precisely what you need with the information in the application.

If commands were the sole aspect of AppleScript, it wouldn't be much more powerful than a macro language. The commands are only the beginning. The three concepts in the next section are what make AppleScript truly powerful as a scripting language.

# Variables

Variables in a scripting language are not like the variables you learned about in high school math or the variable stars you learned about in college astronomy. In AppleScript, variables hold known values to be used in various places in a script. They are place holders for information.

For instance, type in the following script:

```
copy 3 to x
3 + x
```

When you run this script, you'll see that the result window contains the number 6. As far as AppleScript is concerned, it is adding three to three.

In this example, the "copy" command is used to place a value (in this case a number) into a variable named x.

## The Naming of Variables

You access the information in a variable by referring to the name of that variable. A variable can have any name you want to give it, with the following restrictions:

- The name must start with a letter (AppleScript ignores case when looking at variables).

- The name cannot contain characters other than numbers, letters, or underscores (_).

- The name cannot be a reserved word (those words with special meaning to AppleScript). For example, using "copy" for a variable name would cause an error (see figure 2.2), because "copy" means something specific to AppleScript.

```
═══════════ Syntax Error ═══════════
Expected expression but found "copy".

AppleScript English            [ Cancel ]
```

**Figure 2.2**
*You can't use reserved words as variable names.*

Other than reserved names you can call a variable anything you like, however it's probably better to give it a name relevant to what the variable represents. If a script gets a person's age from a database, you could put that information into variable "x," but that wouldn't indicate what that variable contains. A better name for the variable would be "age."

## One more rule

You can't use a variable until you've defined it—that is, put information into it. For instance, run the following script:

```
x + 3
```

AppleScript gives you an error because you attempted to use the variable before it was assigned a value (see figure 2.3).

```
═══════════ Execution Error ═══════════
The variable x is not defined.

AppleScript English            [ Stop ]
```

**Figure 2.3**
*A variable must be assigned a value before it can be used.*

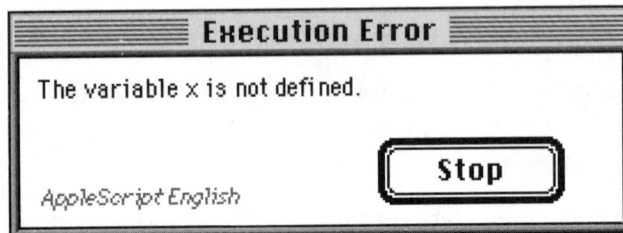

Assigning a value to a variable is called "declaring" it. You can declare a variable with the copy command, as you saw above, or with the set command, as in:

```
set x to 3
```

The set and copy commands have different effects on a variable. "Copying" a variable ensures that the value will remain unchanged unless you act on it with another command. "Setting" a variable, on the other hand, places a value from a specified source into the variable and changes the variable whenever the source changes. You should use the copy command unless you *need* the set command to link a variable to a changing source. (If you are already familiar with programming you may recognize that the set command is what allows you to create pointers.)

## Different Types of Data

A variable can contain five types of data. These types are text, numbers, Booleans, lists, and records.

You have already seen several of these types of data in the script in the previous section. Here's a look at each type more closely.

## Text

When you set the contents of the first window in Scriptable Text Editor to "My first AppleScript," you were working with text.

A variable can hold any text you wish. You can put the text into the variable yourself, as in this script, where "helloText" is the name of the variable:

```
copy "The Tao of AppleScript" to helloText
```

or you can get information from an application and put it into a variable as in:

```
copy word 1 of window 1 of application "Scriptable Text Editor"
to firstWord
```

Sometimes when working with text, you will want to put two pieces of text (also known as strings) together. This is called "concatenating" two strings. To do this, use the "&" symbol.

```
copy "The Tao" & " of AppleScript" to bookTitle
```

This makes the variable "bookTitle" equal to the text "The Tao of AppleScript."

To use quotes within text in Script Editor, you need to put a backslash before each quote mark since quote marks are understood as the beginning and end of text strings; "Start with the letter \"A\"".

## Numbers

You have already seen numbers used in AppleScript. Your first script, 3 + 3, used numbers.

As you can see from that example, AppleScript provides the ability to do math expressions with numbers. AppleScript provides eight ways for you to manipulate numbers or variables with numbers in them. Table 2.1 shows you how each of the different mathematical operations work.

*Table 2.1*
*These are all the mathematical operations you can apply to a number.*

| Operator | Description | Example |
|----------|-------------|---------|
| * | multiplication | 3 * 3 = 9 |
| + | addition | 3 + 3 = 6 |
| - | subtraction | 3 - 3 = 0 |
| ÷ or / | division | 3 ÷ 3 = 1 |
| div | division without remainder | 10 div 3 = 3 |
| mod | division returning remainder | 10 mod 3 = 1 |
| - | negation | -3 |

One operation may not be enough, however. You may need to perform several mathematical operations on a set of numbers. You can combine mathematical operations with AppleScript, but you need to be aware of how AppleScript handles these operations. When AppleScript sees mathematical symbols, it follows what are called the "orders of precedence." It processes operations in this order:

1. Items within parentheses are dealt with first.

2. The negation symbol (-) is applied to all appropriate numbers.

3. Multiplication and division (including the "mod" and "div" commands seen in table 2.1) is performed from left to right.

4. Addition and subtraction is performed from left to right.

To show how these orders of precedence work, you can write a simple script that converts Fahrenheit temperatures to Celsius. For this conversion, you must first subtract 32 from the Fahrenheit temperature, then multiply the result by 5 and divide it by 9. When you type that into Script Editor and run the script, you get a much different result than you might expect:

```
copy 68 to F
F - 32 * 5 / 9
```

The result *should* be 20 degrees, but it isn't. What is AppleScript doing? First, it looks for any information or operation within parentheses. None are present in this example. Next, it looks for any negation signs. Again, there are none. Then it looks for any multiplication and division operations and performs them, from left to right. This means the script first multiplies 32 and 5, divides the result by 9, then subtracts the result of that operation from the Fahrenheit value. The end result, 50.2, isn't the correct answer to the problem we originally stated.

To correct this, you must have AppleScript subtract 32 from the Fahrenheit value and *then* multiply the result by 5 divided by 9. To do that, use parentheses as follows:

```
copy 68 to F
(F - 32) * 5 / 9
```

Now AppleScript returns the correct answer. It does the operation found in the parentheses first, subtracting 32 from the Fahrenheit temperature, then multiplies that result by 5, and divides by 9.

You can see how important parentheses are when doing math operations. If you are running scripts and not getting the numbers you expect, take a careful look at your mathematical operations and make sure you are following the orders of precedence.

## Booleans

A Boolean is a special kind of variable that can only have one of two values: true and false. You won't put Booleans into variables often, but when you do, it will primarily be as "flags." A flag is a normal variable that acts like a checkbox. You put the true or false value into the variable early on in the script, and use that value to decide which commands to perform, or how to perform them.

Booleans come more into play with conditionals which are discussed in the next section.

## Lists

When you work with many related pieces of data, it becomes inconvenient to make separate variables to hold each piece of information. By providing lists, AppleScript allows you to put multiple pieces of information into a single variable.

To define a list, you must enclose it entirely in braces, {...}. Each item in the list is separated from the others with a comma and a space as in the following:

{1, 2, 3}

An item in a list can be any type of data, even another list. For instance, the following list, with the list {1, 2, 3} within it, is valid in the AppleScript language:

{3, "The Tao of AppleScript", true, {1, 2, 3}}

Since you have multiple pieces of information in a list, it is important to be able to work with the particular items found in that list. AppleScript allows you to do this:

```
copy {3, 4, 5} to theList
set item 1 of theList to 6
theList
```

If you run this script, you'll see that you have created a list, called theList, equal to {6, 4, 5}.

When you copy information from a list, the rules (such as math operations, concatenations, and so forth) for a piece of data apply to that information as well. For instance, you could make a new variable, newVar, equal to the first item in theList plus 80. To do this, a third line is added to your script:

```
copy {3, 4, 5} to theList
set item 1 of theList to 6
copy (item 1 of theList) + 80 to newVar
```

Notice the parentheses around "item 1 of theList." If you leave out the parentheses AppleScript will interpret this internally as item 1 of (theList + 80). The parentheses force AppleScript to first find item 1 of theList and then add that to 80.

You can concatenate two lists the same way you concatenate two strings of text. For instance, {3, 4, 5} & {6, 7} will produce {3, 4, 5, 6, 7}.

## Records

When working with large lists—especially those with different types of data, it is difficult to keep track of the type of each piece. Fortunately, AppleScript has a special type of data called a "record" which facilitates retrieving data from a list.

A record is like a list, with one significant difference. With records, each item has a label to make getting information easier. Instead of using a list such as {22, "Derrick", "Schneider"} and trying to remember which item is which piece of information, you could use a record:

```
copy {age:22, firstName:"Derrick", lastName:"Schneider"} to
personalInfo
```

If you want to get the person's first name from this record, you would then add the following command:

```
copy {age:22, firstName:"Derrick", lastName:"Schneider"} to
personalInfo
get firstName of personalInfo
```

It does not matter where the item is in the list. When you use a label to ask for the information, AppleScript finds it with that label regardless of its location within the record.

You need to be careful when concatenating records. If the same label is used in more than one record, AppleScript will keep only one of the items when you concatenate them. More specifically, it keeps only the data in the record to the left of the leftmost "&" symbol for the repeated label in the new record. For instance:

```
{age:22, firstName:"Derrick", lastName:"Schneider"} & {age:28,
fullName:"Jane Smith"}
```

will produce the following record in the result window:

```
{age:22, firstName:"Derrick", lastName:"Schneider",
fullName:"Jane Smith"}
```

Both records included an age label, but AppleScript kept only the data to the left of the "&" symbol.

You will be using these five types of data in example scripts to come. Your own scripts will eventually incorporate them as well. If you don't feel comfortable with them, do not be *too* worried. You will become more familiar with the data types as you use them in example scripts.

## Coercing Variables

There are times when you need to tell AppleScript to interpret one type of data in a variable as different type. For instance, what would you expect from the following statement?

```
3 & 3
```

Based on what you know of the & symbol, you might expect to get "33." Remember, however, that this symbol only applies to text, lists, and records. This is what you actually get:

{3, 3}

AppleScript took the numbers and placed them in a list. But what if you wanted "33?" You must tell AppleScript to treat the two values as if they were "strings." When you concatenate two values this way, it is done as expected.

Telling AppleScript to interpret one type of data as another is called "coercing" data. The following script works the way you want:

3 **as** string & 3 **as** string

AppleScript will format this as "(3 as string) & 3 as string," even though you didn't use the parentheses. The script tells AppleScript to concatenate 3 and 3—treating each one as if it were a string. The result, "33," is another string. Table 2.2 shows how the different coercions can be used.

| Data Type | Coercion | Result |
|---|---|---|
| string | 3 as string | "3" |
| number | "3.5" as number | 3.5 |
| integer | 3.5 as integer | 3 |
| real number | 3 as real | 3.0 |
| list | 3.5 as list | {3.5} |

*Table 2.2*
*The ways in which you can coerce one type of data to another.*

Usually, you won't need to worry about coercing variables, as AppleScript handles them whenever it can.

## Special Variables

AppleScript provides many special variables which *it* fills and allows you to use. These will be very useful to you as you write scripts. The following are the special variables AppleScript offers.

## result

You have already seen the "result" variable used. AppleScript puts this variable in the result window. Every time you use a command, the returned information is put into the variable "result." If no information is returned, the result variable is set to empty.

For instance, when you write:

```
get the name of window 1 of application "Scriptable Text Editor"
```

If there is an open window in Scriptable Text Editor, AppleScript places the name of window 1 into "result." If you then write:

```
copy 3 to x
```

AppleScript sets "result" to 3. To use this variable, you write "result," as in the following script:

```
get the name of window 1 of application "Scriptable Text Editor"
set paragraph 1 of window 1 of application "Scriptable Text Editor" to result
```

This script takes the name of the first window in Scriptable Text Editor, places this information into result, then sets the first paragraph to the value in "result." Because "set" returns no information, the window "the result" is empty.

## it

The variable "it" is most useful when you want to filter information. How could you set up a command to find every word in a document which contains "ip"? The "whose" and "where" clauses as you have learned them provide no way to do so. The "it" variable makes this possible. For instance:

> **get every** word **of** window 1 **of** application "Scriptable Text Editor" **where it contains** "ip"

The "it" variable stands for the object you are looking at—in this case, the words in the first window in Scriptable Text Editor.

## return, space, and tab

When you enter text into an application, you may want to type in a return, space, or tab. AppleScript provides special variables for these. The written-out form of these words represents the characters you need to use. If you were to write the following:

> **set the** contents **of** window 1 **of** application "Scriptable Text Editor" **to** "text" & return & "more text"

then the contents of window 1 becomes:

    text
    more text

## pi

AppleScript also provides you with the value of pi in a variable. It doesn't use the full number, of course, but uses 3.1415926535898 as an approximation. You can use this if you are calculating such things as the area of a circle, as in:

> **copy** 3 **to** r
> pi * (r * r)

where r is a variable that represents the radius of the circle—in this instance, 3.

Variables give you a lot of power in a script. The capability of storing information and/or changing it frequently is one of the things that separates a scripting language from a macro.

At this point, you have looked only at making scripts go along a straight path. AppleScript also provides you with the capabilities of making decisions within a script and repeatedly looping over parts.

## Conditionals

Conditionals give your script the capability of evaluating information and deciding which commands it will execute based on that evaluation. This allows the script to deal with a wide variety of situations.

A conditional is composed of two parts: the question and the command. Different questions apply depending on the type of data, but for a true condition, the end result will be the same. If the answer to the question is true, then the commands are executed.

Conditionals, also called "if...then" statements, conceptually look like this: if (a certain condition is true) then (do these commands) (see figure 2.4).

**copy** 3 **to** x
**if** x **is** 3 **then** beep

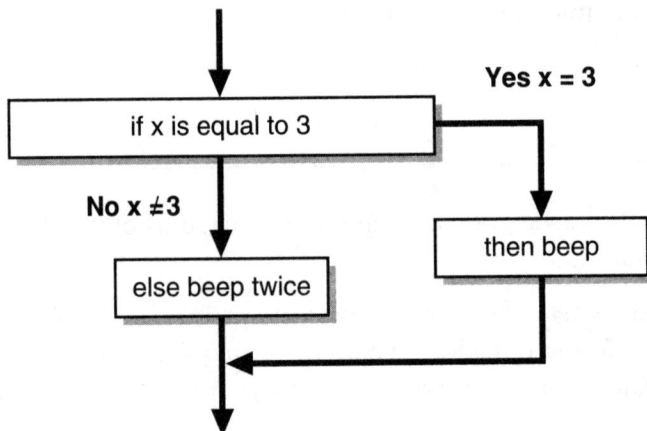

*Figure 2.4*
*The basic "if then"*
*command.*

This script first puts 3 into x, then checks to see if x is equal to 3. Since the condition is true, the script beeps.

Including one command with the conditional is only so powerful. A more complex form allows you to include multiple commands in the conditional:

```
copy 3 to x
if x is 3 then
    beep
    set the contents of window 1 of application "Scriptable
    Text Editor" to "The Tao of AppleScript"
end if
```

In this form, the conditional (including "then") goes on one line. The next lines include all the commands you want to include within that conditional. The "end if" tells AppleScript to include all the commands between it and the conditional. Any commands after the "end if" are not dependent on the conditional. AppleScript provides a visual cue by formatting these as indented text between the conditional and the "end if."

The commands inside a conditional can be anything—even another conditional, as in:

```
copy 3 to x
copy 5 to q
if x is 3 then
    if q is 5 then beep
    set the contents of window 1 of application "Scriptable
    Text Editor" to "The Tao of AppleScript"
    beep
end if
```

Putting a conditional inside a conditional or a repeat loop within a repeat loop is called "nesting."

These are the two basic forms of the conditional. Before moving on to more complex forms, take a minute to look at the different methods of comparing two pieces of data in the conditional.

## Comparisons

Conditionals are one of the most useful ways of comparing two pieces of data. Perhaps the most basic question you can ask about the relationship between two pieces of data is, "Is this data equal to that data?" AppleScript has the capability of making that comparison with the "=" symbol or the word "is," as in the following examples:

---

**copy** 3 **to** x

---

**if** x = 3 **then** beep

---

**if** x **is** 3 **then** beep

---

Both these lines do the same thing: If x is equal to 3, then beep.

Another comparison is, "Is this piece of data different from that piece of data?" To perform this, AppleScript, uses the "≠" symbol (made by typing Option-=) or the words "is not."

---

**copy 4 to** x
**if** x ≠ 3 **then** beep
**if** x **is not** 3 **then** beep

---

Within a conditional, you can write the contraction "isn't" in place of "is not." When AppleScript compiles the script, it will expand your contraction to "is not."

These commands say "if x isn't equal to 3, then beep."

You can always compare two pieces of data to determine whether or not they are equal. However, some types of data can be compared in ways unique to their type. Using these specialized comparisons gives you the capability to evaluate a wide range of information.

## Text

With strings of text, you may not want to look at whether or not one piece of text is *equal* to another. You may want to evaluate part of the text to see if it meets certain criteria. AppleScript provides five ways of doing this, illustrated below.

---

**if** "The Tao of AppleScript" **starts with** "Th" **then** beep

---

**if** "The Tao of AppleScript" **ends with** "ipt" **then** beep

---

**if** "The Tao of AppleScript" **contains** "Apple" **then** beep

---

**if** "The Tao of AppleScript" **comes before** "Zz" **then** beep

---

**if** "The Tao of AppleScript" **comes after** "Aa" **then** beep

---

The "comes before" and "comes after" comparisons use alphabetical order to determine whether the comparison is true or false.

## Numbers

Numbers use the methods of comparisons you would expect. In AppleScript, you can determine if one number is greater than another (>), less than another (<), greater than or equal to another (≥, Option-period), or less than or equal to another (≤, Option-comma).

The following conditionals are all true and will therefore result in beeps:

---

**copy** 4 **to** x
**if** x > 3 **then** beep
**if** x < 5 **then** beep
**if** x ≥ 4 **then** beep
**if** x ≤ 6 **then** beep

---

## Lists

With a list, you can use "starts with," "ends with," and "contains" just as you can when comparing text strings. However, they work a little differently.

Look at the following conditionals:

---

**if** {1, 2, 3} **starts with** {1} **then** beep

---

For this comparison to be true, the item must be an entire element of that list or record. For instance:

---

**if** {"My", 2, 3} **starts with** {"M"} **then** beep

---

This will not beep because while *item* 1 of the second list starts with "M," the *list* starts with "My".

Elements must also be referenced in order of their sequence within the set. When you ask about multiple elements in a list, the elements you're asking for must be in the same order as they appear in the list. For instance, look at the following example:

---

**if** {1, 2, 3, 4} **contains** {2, 4} **then** beep

---

This conditional will not be true because {2, 4} isn't in {1, 2, 3, 4}, even though both elements of {2, 4} are found in the list.

## Records

When comparing records, both the label and the data with that label must be equal. If in the following script, you were to inquire about the label "age," the data assigned to that label, "22," would need to be equal as well:

---

**if** {age:22, firstName:"Derrick", lastName:"Schneider"} **contains** {age:22, lastName:"Schneider"} **then** beep

---

This script will result in a beep even though "age" and "lastName" are not sequential. Records are not limited to sequential order as lists are. The script above returns a true because those items are included in the record; their order makes no difference.

## Booleans

Booleans are limited to the comparisons "equal to" and "not equal to." Here are some examples of conditionals using Booleans—each script will beep, as all cases return a true from the comparisons:

```
copy true to theflag
if theflag = true then beep
if theflag ≠ false then beep
```

The terms "equal to" and "not equal to" can be written in many forms, such as =, ≠; is equal to, is not equal to; equals, does not equal; and is, is not. AppleScript will understand any of them.

## Modifiers

There are times when you'll want to modify how a comparison will be carried out. For instance, you may want to look for the opposite condition, do multiple comparisons, or even override some of the ways AppleScript looks at data to make a more specific comparison. AppleScript provides ways to do all these things.

### and, or, not

Sometimes a single comparison will not provide what you need. You may need more flexibility or power.

For instance, what if you want to know if an item *isn't* a certain value? The modifier "not" enables you to reverse the results of the comparison.

You might have the following:

```
copy 4 to x
if not (x is 3) then beep
```

When AppleScript executes this script, it first evaluates the comparison inside the parentheses. If x isn't three, then this part of the comparison is false. When AppleScript sees the word "not," however, it reverses the result of the comparison. In AppleScript's eyes, this conditional is now true, and it will beep.

AppleScript enables you to do multiple comparisons using the "and" and "or" modifiers. With "and," AppleScript requires all comparisons to be true before it executes the commands. The "or" modifier checks to see if any one of the comparisons is true. If any one is true, the commands are executed.

Imagine that you only want to execute a command if a list starts with a bullet (•) and is more than three items long.

You could do this by nesting two conditionals, as follows:

```
copy {"•", 4, 5, 6} to x
if x starts with {"•"} then
    if the number of items in x > 3 then
        beep
    end if
end if
```

This script looks at the list in x and determines whether or not it starts with a bullet. If a true is returned, it then looks at the second conditional and determines if there are more than three items in x. If true again, the commands are executed.

This can be cumbersome, however. A simpler way is to use the "and" modifier, as follows:

```
copy {"•", 4, 5, 6} to x
if (x starts with "•") and (the number of items in x > 3) then
    beep
end if
```

This script does the same thing as the previous one. AppleScript looks at the first comparison, then the second. If both are true, the commands are executed. If either is false, they are not.

The "or" modifier works similarly, but differs in the results. In the above example, an "or" modifier would mean that the commands will be executed as long as one of the comparisons is true. If the list has more than three items, but doesn't start with a "•," the commands will be executed.

These three modifiers may be used in any combination. You could create the following script:

```
copy 4 to x
copy 4 to y
copy 7 to z
if ((x > 3) and (y < 5)) or (not (z > 6)) then beep
```

This conditional will only be true if z is not greater than 6 *or* if x is greater than 3 and y is less than 5.

When using multiple modifiers, remember that each comparison that is modified must be within its own set of parentheses. Looking at the above conditional, the "or" modifier requires that both comparisons be in parentheses. This is why additional parentheses were placed around the entire "and" comparison and the entire "not" comparison in addition to the individual "and" and "or" comparisons.

## considering and ignoring

Though AppleScript provides a wide array of comparisons, sometimes they don't do exactly what you need them to. For instance, AppleScript doesn't pay attention to uppercase and lowercase characters. "Apple" and "apple" are exactly the same to AppleScript.

This could be a problem for some scripts. Fortunately, AppleScript is capable of overriding some of these factors with the "considering" and "ignoring" modifiers. Compare the following two scripts:

```
if "Apple" is "apple" then beep
```

```
considering case
    if "Apple" is "apple" then beep
end considering
```

Both of these scripts seem to pose the same question, but the second instructs AppleScript to "consider" the case of the text when executing the comparison. The second script will not beep.

The "end considering" command tells AppleScript where this rule applies.

The opposite of "considering" is "ignoring." This tells AppleScript to stop paying attention to a certain condition. Again, look at the following scripts, where the first instance of the word "AppleScript" is written with a space between the words:

```
if "Apple Script" is "AppleScript" then beep
```

```
ignoring white space
    if "Apple Script" is "AppleScript" then beep
end ignoring
```

Under normal circumstances, AppleScript considers a space to be a character; therefore, the first script does not beep. With the "ignoring" command however, AppleScript will "see" only the actual letters—not the space.

Table 2.3 illustrates all the options with the "considering" and "ignoring" modifiers and indicates what AppleScript would do if left unmodified.

| Term | What it stands for | Example | AppleScript's default |
|---|---|---|---|
| case | the difference between upper and lower case | "Apple" vs. "apple" | Ignored |
| white space | returns, spaces, and tabs | "Apple Script" vs. "AppleScript" | Considered |
| diacriticals | ^,¨,´,`,' | "résumé" vs. "resume" | Considered |
| hyphens | - | "half-hour" vs. "halfhour" | Considered |
| punctuation | any punctuation mark | "Wow!" vs. "Wow" | Considered |

If you want to combine several different options, you can use "and" and "but." Look at the following script:

*Table 2.3*
*The various options for "considering" and "ignoring."*

---

**considering** case **but ignoring** white space **and** diacriticals

    **if** "the resume" **is** "therésumé" **then** beep

**end considering**

---

This script will beep. With these comparisons and modifiers, commands are executed only when certain conditions are met. This allows for very complex decisions within a script.

## else statements

You have seen that a conditional instructs a script to continue when the comparison returns a true. However, you may want to execute some commands if a conditional returns a true (if x is equal to 3) and other commands if it doesn't (if x is not equal to 3). In AppleScript, the else statement makes this possible.

---

**copy** 4 **to** x

**if** x **is** 3 **then**

    beep

**else**

    beep 2

**end if**

---

35

With this script, AppleScript first checks to see if x is equal to 3. If so, the script executes the commands normally, continuing on to commands that come after the "end if" statement.

If x is not equal to 3, however, AppleScript sees the "else" statement and runs the commands under *that* portion of the script. When those commands are finished, AppleScript proceeds to commands after the "end if."

You can put conditionals on "else" statements. Suppose you want to get a number from a database (1, 2, 3, or 4), and you want to run different commands for the different numbers. The script would look like this:

```
copy 4 to x
if x is 1 then
    beep
else if x is 2 then
    beep 2
else if x is 3 then
    beep 3
else
    beep 4
end if
```

As before, the script first looks at the original conditional—if x is equal to 1, it executes those commands and continues with the script after the "end if" statement. If x does not equal 1, it will start looking through the "else" commands. If x is 2, it will execute the commands under that "else" command and continue with the script. If not, it will go on to check if x is equal to 3 and go through the same steps. Finally, if x isn't 1, 2, or 3, then it must be 4; the commands under the final "else" statement are run, as none of the previous conditions were met.

You will use conditionals frequently in your own scripting, particularly in scripts that must be aware of potential problems or changing values. With these capabilities, your scripts can deal with any conditions you anticipate.

## Repeat Loops

While the capability of branching in different directions is certainly useful, it doesn't provide all the power a scripting language needs.

Repeat loops are the real workhorses of the AppleScript language. They allow you to automate big, repetitive tasks. As the name implies, a repeat loop performs a set of commands over and over again.

Just as AppleScript gives you many options for comparing data, it also gives you many ways to repeat sets of commands.

## Basic Repeat Loops

A basic repeat loop is one which simply goes on forever, until stopped by an outside influence, such as a person running the script. The following example shows one such loop:

```
copy "The Tao of AppleScript" to helloText
repeat
    set the contents of window 1 of application "Scriptable
    Text Editor" to the contents of window 1 of application
    "Scriptable Text Editor" & helloText & return
end repeat
```

In this case, you're telling AppleScript to add "The Tao of AppleScript" and a return character to the end of the current contents of the window. Note that, just as with "end if," "end repeat" tells AppleScript which commands to be repeated.

Run this script, and use the application menu to bring Scriptable Text Editor to the front. You will see that the script is dutifully repeating the line "The Tao of AppleScript." This would continue indefinitely were it not for the fact that Scriptable Text

Editor will give you an error when the document size reaches 32 Kilobytes.

The only way to stop this script otherwise is to go back to Script Editor, using the application menu, and click on the "Stop" button (or type Command-period while in Script Editor). *Rarely* will you want a script to continue forever. AppleScript provides you with the "exit" command for exiting a repeat loop in a script.

The next script is the same as the previous one, but now exits the repeat loop when there are ten paragraphs in Scriptable Text Editor:

```
copy "The Tao of AppleScript" to helloText
repeat
    if the number of paragraphs of window 1 of application
    "Scriptable Text Editor" ≥ 10 then exit repeat
    set the contents of window 1 of application "Scriptable
    Text Editor" to the contents of window 1 of application
    "Scriptable Text Editor" & helloText & return
end repeat
```

In this case, the first command in the repeat loop is a conditional that asks if there are ten or more paragraphs in the first window. If there are, then it executes the exit command which tells the script to go to the command immediately following the "end repeat."

While you could do anything you need to with this repeat loop and the various conditionals, it would require a great deal of cumbersome work. AppleScript provides mechanisms for constructing more complex repeat loops.

## Conditional Repeat Loops

A key feature of repeat loops is the capability to exit them when they've done their job. In the previous section, you saw how you can use a conditional and the "exit" command to do this.

However, AppleScript uses two specialized repeat loops, "repeat while" and "repeat until," to make the task easier.

The following script uses the "repeat until" loop to achieve the same effect as the script in the previous section:

```
copy "The Tao of AppleScript" to helloText
repeat until the number of paragraphs in window 1 of
application "Scriptable Text Editor" ≥ 10
    set the contents of window 1 of application "Scriptable
    Text Editor" to the contents of window 1 of application
    "Scriptable Text Editor" & helloText & return
end repeat
```

For each loop, the script checks to see if there are 10 or more paragraphs in the first window within Scriptable Text Editor. If so, it does not execute the commands within the repeat loop, but goes to commands found after the "end repeat."

AppleScript also has a "repeat while" command, as in the following script:

```
copy "The Tao of AppleScript" to helloText
repeat while the number of paragraphs in window 1 of
application "Scriptable Text Editor" < 10
    set the contents of window 1 of application "Scriptable
    Text Editor" to the contents of window 1 of application
    "Scriptable Text Editor" & helloText & return
end repeat
```

This script does the same thing as the previous scripts, but differs in semantics. Now it says "as long as there are less than ten paragraphs in the first window, do these commands." The two repeat loops are functionally equivalent. The one you use depends on which makes more sense to you.

## Counting Repeat Loops

You may want to make a repeat loop run a certain number of times and *then* exit. You can do that by using an incrementing variable and checking the value of that variable each time through the loop, as in the following script:

```
copy "The Tao of AppleScript" to helloText
copy 1 to x
repeat while x < 10
    set the contents of window 1 of application "Scriptable
    Text Editor" to the contents of window 1 of application
    "Scriptable Text Editor" & helloText & return
    copy x + 1 to x
end repeat
```

The loop will continue to run as long as x is less than 10.

A simpler way to do this would be to use the command "repeat _ times" (where the underscore is a placeholder for a variable) as follows:

```
copy "The Tao of AppleScript" to helloText
repeat 10 times
    set the contents of window 1 of application "Scriptable
    Text Editor" to the contents of window 1 of application
    "Scriptable Text Editor" & helloText & return
end repeat
```

The "repeat _ times" command tells AppleScript to do whatever commands are found inside the repeat loop a specified number of times and then continue with the commands after the "end repeat."

However, you may need to know how far the script is through the loop. To do this, AppleScript provides a different repeat loop, the "repeat with _ from" loop. The following script shows how it's used:

```
copy "The Tao of AppleScript" to helloText
repeat with i from 1 to 10
    set the contents of window 1 of application "Scriptable
    Text Editor" to the contents of window 1 of application
    "Scriptable Text Editor" & helloText & return
end repeat
```

The repeat loop declares a "counting variable" (i) and adds 1 to the value of that variable each time it goes through the loop, until that variable equals 10.

The counting variable follows the same rules as normal variables, except that it does not need to be declared beforehand.

With just these conditions, this counting variable would pose a problem if you wanted to increase it by more than 1 at a time. What if you want the counting variable to be increased by 10, or some other number, each pass?

Just as you can modify conditionals, AppleScript provides a modifier for this type of repeat loop as well. The "by" modifier tells AppleScript by what amount the counting variable will be increased each time.

```
copy "The Tao of AppleScript" to helloText
repeat with i from 1 to 10 by 2
    set the contents of window 1 of application "Scriptable
    Text Editor" to the contents of window 1 of application
    "Scriptable Text Editor" & helloText & return
end repeat
```

You can use the "by" modifier to count down as well as up. Suppose you want the variable to start out at 100 and end at 1. To do this, you could use the following command:

```
repeat with x from 100 to 1 by -1
end repeat
```

This tells AppleScript to count down by 1 each time through the loop. You could use -10 if you wanted the script to count down by 10 instead of 1.

## Traversing a list

The last kind of repeat loop allows you to "traverse a list." Running a set of commands once for every item in a list is called "traversing." You might want to execute a set of commands for every paragraph in a document, in which case you would be traversing the paragraphs in the document. A traverse loop runs once for every value in a list, setting the counting variable to that item in the list. For instance, if you wanted a script that filled in people's names in a form letter, this repeat loop traverses a list:

```
repeat with i in {"Derrick", "John", "Mary"}
    beep
end repeat
```

With this repeat loop the commands will run and therefore beep three times. On the first pass, the variable i will equal "Derrick"; the second pass "John"; etc.

Traversing is a powerful tool. For complex scripts you will find that this is a technique you will frequently use. Later, we'll look at how to traverse directories in the Finder, giving you the ability to do some very powerful file manipulation.

## On Your Own

This chapter has covered the tools and equipment you'll need for your journey—the mechanics of the AppleScript language. Just as important, however, is knowing where you are going and what route you will take to get there. You'll need a strategy for building a script from scratch.

In the next section are several approaches to building a simple script. From there you can move on to more complex, real-world types of scripts.

Before moving on, make sure to take a break and play with some of these concepts. Become familiar with the different aspects of AppleScript. Have some fun!

# *Finding Your Way*

Now that you've had a look at the mechanics of AppleScript and its language, you need to learn how to go about writing an actual script to achieve a specific goal. In this section you'll write a script step by step that creates a window and moves it around the screen. Once written, it will be refined and added to, making it simpler and more powerful. These steps are the same development procedure used by programmers to write code—they will become part of your own scripting style with a little practice.

## Moving a Window in Scriptable Text Editor

The window-moving script that you are about to write is a good example of how even the simplest script is the end result of a series of improvements. The ultimate goal is to move the first window in Scriptable Text Editor across and down your Mac's screen in a specific pattern. To achieve that goal, you must think of each part of the script, one at a time, and build on those aspects.

THE TAO OF APPLESCRIPT

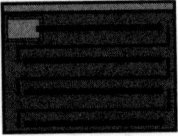

The path the
moving window
will take.

## Get the Basics in Place

Before you start any script, you should take a moment to decide
what that script's key components are. In this case, the script's
most basic object is a window in Scriptable Text Editor, and the
most basic function of the script is setting the position of that
window. So, you must begin by addressing this main object and
setting its position.

Since Scriptable Text Editor automatically opens a window
whenever it is launched, you won't need to tell it to do so.

You may want to see the script's actions so you can understand
how it operates. To do this use the "activate" command. Activate
brings an application to the front or launches an application if it
isn't already running.

---

activate application "Scriptable Text Editor"

---

This script's single line brings the application to the forefront.

## Using Tell

Since you will be working in Scriptable Text Editor throughout
this script, the "tell" command will provide a useful shortcut. You
can use the "tell" command to let AppleScript know that until
further notice, you want all commands directed to that application—instead of referring to Scriptable Text Editor in every line to
address the specific window. Using the tell command gives a
certain amount of visual structure to your script as well. At this
stage, it may seem like overkill to add extra commands and make
it even longer, but as you fill out your script it will make sense.
Your script will now look like this:

---

**tell** application "Scriptable Text Editor'
    activate
**end tell**

---

A tell command must always include an "end tell" to let
AppleScript know you have finished directing commands to that
application.

Your first step will be to set the position of the window to some arbitrary coordinates on the screen, say {100,100}. The {100,100} represents the values of the x- and y-coordinates, relative to the upper left corner of the Mac's screen {0,0}.

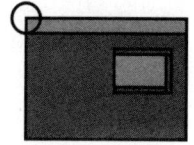

The origin (0,0) point of the Mac screen.

```
tell application "Scriptable Text Editor"
    activate
    set the position of window 1 to {100, 100}
end tell
```

## Using Variables

The end result of the next script will be a window that moves across the screen. To accomplish this, the position of the window will need to be changed repeatedly. When dealing with values that you want to change frequently it is best to replace those numbers with variables. Remember, however, that you cannot use a variable without defining it first. Therefore, you'll need to modify your script in two ways: replace the numbers defining the coordinates of the window with variables, and add the necessary lines to define those variables.

Start by simply defining the variables and replacing the coordinates with them, and deal with getting the variables to change later.

The script will now look like this:

```
copy 100 to y
copy 100 to x
tell application "Scriptable Text Editor"
    activate
    set the position of window 1 to {x, y}
end tell
```

The copy commands place the number 100 into the variables x and y. Since these commands are not being applied specifically

47

to the application Scriptable Text Editor, they don't need to be within the tell command. Run the script. Nothing will appear to work differently, but it is now using variables to execute the commands.

In order for the window to move, the values of the variables will need to change. To do this you'll need to replace the copy commands (that define the variables as a single number with repeat loops) (that will increase the values of the variables for each pass through the repeat loop).

The script will start by moving the window across the top of the screen, left to right, then back to the left side of the screen, down a notch, and across again. To do this, you will need to put one loop inside the other. The first loop increments the value of y; the second loop increments the value of x. Every time the window moves down a notch, the script will move the window across the screen. Here's how the resulting script looks:

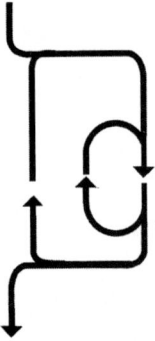

A repeat loop within a repeat loop.

```
repeat with y from 0 to 480
    repeat with x from 0 to 640
        tell application "Scriptable Text Editor"
            activate
            set the position of window 1 to {x, y}
        end tell
    end repeat
end repeat
```

The first line of the script tells AppleScript to step, or repeat, from 0 to 480 and put each number it steps through into the variable y. Then, for each step of y, it steps from 0 to 640 and places each number it steps through into the variable x. Thus, when x has incremented 640 times, y will increment once. Each time y increments, the variable x increments 640 times again.

The "movement" of the window is produced by the set command, which treats the values of the incrementing x and y variables as screen coordinates, telling the application to place the window at these coordinates.

While stepping through each number, the script instructs Scriptable Text Editor to change the position of the window to x pixels from the left of the screen and y pixels from the top of the screen. As the script progresses, the window is placed at the position {0,0}, then {1,0}, then {2,0}, and so forth. When the window reaches the position {640,0}, the inner repeat loop finishes and passes through its end repeat statement; the script loops back to the initial repeat and y increments by 1, then starts the inner repeat loop all over again.

Run the script again.

You may notice that the script has some flaws in the way it works. While it does exactly what you told it to, it's not really what was intended. The window doesn't stay within the screen's edges, it starts out covered by the menu bar, and it goes so slowly! You may have also noticed that the window keeps insisting it should come to the front when you try to interrupt the script and go back to Script Editor. This is because the activate command is placed within the repeat loop. Though this is not exactly a spectacular initial script, these problems are easy to fix with a little work.

## Fine Tuning

To prevent the script from constantly pushing itself to the front, you should get the activate command where it belongs. Since the activate command is directed to Scriptable Text Editor, you can't simply put activate at the beginning of the script, as it would fall outside the tell command. You will have to move the tell command itself.

This script assumes that you have a standard Apple 13" or 14" monitor. You may want to adjust your values if you have a different screen size.

Mac Plus, SE, SE/30, Classic, or Color 12":
512 x 384

PowerBook:
640 x 400

To stop the script before it finishes (as it will take a long time to finish) click on Script Editor and press Stop (or press Command-period).

```
tell application "Scriptable Text Editor"
    activate
        repeat with y from 0 to 480
            repeat with x from 0 to 640
                set the position of window 1 to {x, y}
            end repeat
        end repeat
end tell
```

The easiest way to speed it up is to put a "by" modifier in the repeat loops. Instead of increasing x and y by a single pixel each time it repeats, you can increase it by 25. The by modifier goes right where you would expect it to in a regular sentence:

```
tell application "Scriptable Text Editor"
    activate
        repeat with y from 0 to 480 by 25
            repeat with x from 0 to 640 by 25
                set the position of window 1 to {x, y}
            end repeat
        end repeat
end tell
```

The coordinates used for the position of a window are located *below* the title bar in the upper left corner of the window.

Next, let's have the window start within the visible area of the Mac's screen. The window will need to be placed below the menu bar, which extends 20 pixels from the top of the screen. You also have to take into account the title bar of the window, which is another 20 pixels.

You don't need to change the initial x-coordinate, because it already falls within the visible area. However, you will need to change the initial y-coordinate so that it positions the window 40 pixels down from the top edge of the screen. To do that, you must change the range of numbers in the first repeat loop.

```
tell application "Scriptable Text Editor"
    activate
    repeat with y from 40 to 480 by 25
        repeat with x from 0 to 640 by 25
            set the position of window 1 to {x, y}
        end repeat
    end repeat
end tell
```

Take a moment to run the script now. You'll see that your small changes have made it work much better.

The third flaw in the initial script is that the window goes all the way off the screen. To fix this problem, you'll need to change the upper limit of the repeat loops so that the window doesn't move as far.

How far should the window move? Well, you don't know because you don't know how big the window is; you only know the coordinates of the upper left corner. To solve this, you'll need to set the size of the window. This is called setting its "bounds" property. The bounds property is a list of numbers that look like this: {100,100,300,400}. The first number is the distance from the left edge of the screen to the left edge of the window; the second is the distance from the top of the screen to the top text entry area of the window (these first two numbers are also the numbers used by AppleScript to define the position of the window); the third item is the distance from the left edge of the screen to the right edge of the window, and the fourth item is the distance from the top of the screen to the bottom of the window. To make the window 100 pixels high and 200 pixels wide using the coordinates from the last example, you would use the command:

```
set the bounds of window 1 to {0, 40, 200, 140}
```

This command sets the *position* of the window to {0,40} and sets the *bounds* of that window to 100 pixels by 200 pixels from those coordinates. Since you now know the window is exactly 100 pixels wide and 200 pixels high, you can set the repeat loops' values so that the window stops 100 pixels from the right edge and 200 pixels short of the bottom edge of the screen. This will limit the window's movement to 380 on the y axis and 440 on the x axis. As you run the script you'll see that all of the basic flaws have been corrected.

```
tell application "Scriptable Text Editor"
    activate
    set the bounds of window 1 to {0, 40, 200, 140}
    repeat with y from 40 to 380 by 25
        repeat with x from 0 to 440 by 25
            set the position of window 1 to {x, y}
        end repeat
    end repeat
end tell
```

## Fix the Bugs

No matter how much you think about a script, there will almost always be a problem you didn't foresee. Worse yet, the script that runs flawlessly on your machine may break the first time you run it on someone else's computer. Such are the realities of scripting.

While you cannot avoid every problem, you should take some time to prevent as many as possible. Bugs are usually the result of assumptions that shouldn't have been made. You should strive to expand your thinking to include what might happen when someone else uses the script.

Since Scriptable Text Editor makes a window when it starts, you didn't have to—but what if there wasn't one? What would have happened to your script? To find out, launch Scriptable Text Editor if it isn't running already, and close all of its windows. Now run your script again.

It's obvious what went wrong. The script can't "get" a window if there is no window to get (see figure 3.1). To make sure that the user doesn't get this error, the first thing you need to do is to check that there is at least one open window. To do this, you must set up a conditional. Use the conditional to see if there are any open windows, and make one if there aren't. In this case the conditional will need to check if there isn't a window. To do this, you'll need to use the "not" modifier. You need to say, "If it is *not* the case that there is a window 1, then make one."

**Figure 3.1**
*The inevitable bug: If a window isn't open, Script Editor will show you this dialog box.*

The script version of this looks like this:

```
tell application "Scriptable Text Editor"
    activate
    if not (window 1 exists) then make window
    set the bounds of window 1 to {0, 40, 200, 140}
    repeat with y from 40 to 380 by 25
        repeat with x from 0 to 440 by 25
            set the position of window 1 to {x, y}
        end repeat
    end repeat
end tell
```

If there is an open window, then there is a window 1, since the definition of window 1 in AppleScript *is* the frontmost window.

## Add New Features

Halfway through the development of a script you may think of new features to add. This can lead to "featuritis," where you never quite finish the script, but keep adding new features. It can, however, also be an important phase in the development of your script and your scripting abilities.

New features can make your script more impressive and more practical to other people if you ever plan on sharing your script creations with other AppleScript users. Features can range from aesthetic ("mag wheels," as my father would call them) to functional.

Even this simple script could have features added to it. For example, if you want to know exactly where the window is at any moment, you could tell the script to put the position of the window into the window itself.

You can get the window's x and y coordinates fairly easily since you've already put them into variables. To put those numbers in the window together, you need to concatenate them. However, since they are numbers, you need to tell AppleScript to treat them as text. Putting all this together: you need to set the contents of the window to the values of x and y as text, separated by a comma.

The script now looks like this:

```
tell application "Scriptable Text Editor"
        activate
        if not (window 1 exists) then make window at beginning
        set the bounds of window 1 to {0, 40, 200, 140}
        repeat with y from 40 to 380 by 25
                repeat with x from 0 to 440 by 25
                        set the position of window 1 to {x, y}
                        set the contents of window 1 to (x as string) & "," &
                        (y as string)
                end repeat
        end repeat
end tell
```

When you run the script, you will see that it behaves exactly the way you intended. Congratulations! You've written your first complex script! Though moving a window around your Mac's screen may not be the be-all end-all of scripting with AppleScript, it does show you the principles involved in creating a script from scratch.

## On Your Own

If you want to practice some scripts on your own, feel free to take a break. Perhaps you thought of some other feature that you would like to add to this script, or maybe you'd like to try making the window move in a different pattern. The point is that you should explore AppleScript on your own and be creative about what you want to do with it.

# Chapter 4
# Building Scripts

# Living off the Land

This next script is actually somewhat functional. Unlike the window moving script, this script manipulates data—probably one of the aspects of AppleScript you'll use most.

The script numbers lines of text in a window. Though some word processors have this feature, Scriptable Text Editor isn't one of them. But because it's AppleScript aware, you can make a script that will do it for you.

You'll need to do a little bit of setup beforehand. Launch Scriptable Text Editor; it will automatically make a new window for you. In that window, put four lines of text as in figure 4.1a—you can write whatever you like. The second window (see figure 4.1b) shows how that same window will look after you have run the script on it.

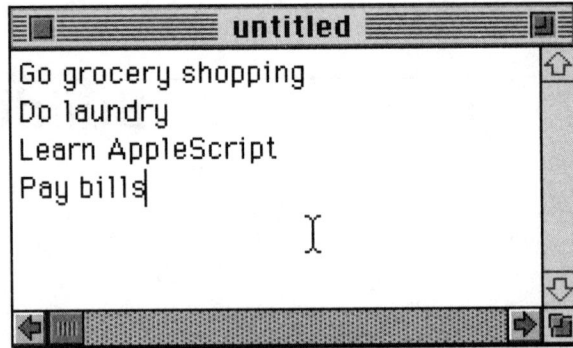

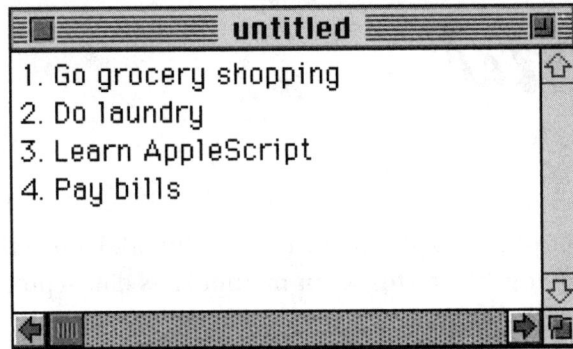

## Get the Basics Working

Next, think about what some of the key commands will be.
Obviously, the most important line of this script will be the one
that puts the appropriate number in front of the line of text.
You've seen how the "make" command in Scriptable Text Editor
can create an object with certain properties. The make command
may also be used to make an object with a certain value, that you
define. Since you will be addressing the application Scriptable Text

Editor, this command enables you to make a word with the value "1. " (note the space after the period). This is how you will create the numbers that will be added to the lines of text. (Since a return follows each line in the window, the lines are actually separate paragraphs.)

```
tell window 1 of application "Scriptable Text Editor"
        activate
        make word at beginning of paragraph 1 with data "1. "
end tell
```

The number you'll place in front of the paragraph will change depending on which paragraph the script is working with. You will need to make this number a variable, and that means you'll need to define the variable.

The script uses a repeat loop to increment the variable, one integer at a time. In order for the script to know how high to count, tell it to count the number of paragraphs in the window and make that number the maximum value of the repeat loop. Finally, concatenate that number with a period followed by a space (for aesthetic reasons). The resulting script looks like this:

```
tell window 1 of application "Scriptable Text Editor"
    repeat with i from 1 to the number of paragraphs
        activate
        make word at beginning of paragraph i with data (i as
        string) & ". "
    end repeat
end tell
```

## Make It Better

Though this script works correctly, there are ways to improve it. Further enhancements can include annotating the script and making sure it will work under unexpected circumstances.

## Comments

After you've been scripting for a while, you'll find yourself looking back over your old scripts. Unfortunately, it becomes difficult to remember why you used certain commands in a complex script. To help yourself, remember AppleScript provides a mechanism for leaving yourself notes, called "comments," in a script. These comments will also be useful to others who may use your script.

There are two ways to make comments. The first is to precede the information with two hyphens (--). AppleScript ignores all the information in a line after two hyphens. A comment can be either an entire line or at the end of a line, as long as you precede it with two hyphens. For example:

```
tell window 1 of application "Scriptable Text Editor"
    repeat with i from 1 to the number of paragraphs
        --This repeat loop numbers the paragraphs
        activate
        make word at beginning of paragraph i with data (i as
        string) & ". " --i is a number so needs to be coerced to a
        string
    end repeat
end tell
```

You may also want a comment that spans several lines. While you could do this by "commenting out" line after line, AppleScript provides an easier mechanism for making multi-line comments. Putting the characters "(*" and "*)" at the beginning and end of text makes AppleScript ignore everything between them. The following example shows how this looks:

```
(* This script numbers all the paragraphs in the first window in
Scriptable Text Editor

 It also uses the make command from Scriptable Text Editor to insert
the new word *)
```

```
tell window 1 of application "Scriptable Text Editor"
    repeat with i from 1 to the number of paragraphs --This is a
    comment after a line
        --This repeat loop numbers the paragraphs
        activate
        make word at beginning of paragraph i with data (i as
        string) & ". " --remember to make i into a string because i
        is a number
    end repeat
end tell
```

There are no rules for how many comments may be put into a script. Some people comment on every line, defining each command, while others use them infrequently, only to define sections of script. Remember, these comments are for you or perhaps someone looking at your script, so only you can decide how many to include.

There are a few guidelines about where different types of comments should be placed. A comment at the end of a line is best for making a special note about that line. In the example above, the comment on the line containing the "make" command is there to note that the variable i must be coerced to a string.

A comment on its own line explains the commands following it. These types of comments are placed before a chain of events to explain its purpose. In the example, the comment on a line by itself explains the purpose of the following repeat loop.

Finally, multi-paragraph comments go at the beginning to explain the entire script, perhaps as a technical overview.

Each script also has a comment area at the top of Script Editor's window, that area is used to describe the overall function of a script to a prospective user.

Proper commenting enables you to come back to scripts much later and easily understand what you did and why. In addition to helping you to understand the script, commenting makes it easier to look into a script and pull out parts to use in other scripts.

## Interface

If you plan to distribute your script to other AppleScript users, it's important to consider how they will see your script. How an uninitiated user interacts with your script, or for that matter how your script interacts with the user, can make a big difference in how elegant your script seems.

Look back at the window-moving script. While the "activate" command could have gone anywhere in the script, it was put at the beginning to let you see what the script was doing, so that all the script's actions would be clear to you. However, to someone using the script, seeing a window being made and sized can appear jerky and unrefined. If you place the activate command later in the script, the application is brought forward with the window already set up, and the window begins moving right away.

Someone using the paragraph numbering script is likely to want to go back to the document that was just numbered, so you may want to include the activate command to bring that window to the front automatically. If you put the activate command just before the end of the tell command, so it is the last action executed, the script will run in the background and the user will see the window only when the script is finished. The script looks like this:

---

*(\* This script numbers all the paragraphs in the first window in Scriptable Text Editor*

 *It uses the make command from Scriptable Text Editor to insert the new word \*)*

**tell** window 1 **of** application "Scriptable Text Editor"

    **repeat with** i **from** 1 **to the** number **of** paragraphs

        *--This repeat loop numbers the paragraphs*

        make word at **beginning of** paragraph i with data (i **as** string) & ". " *--i is a number so needs to be coerced to a string*

```
    end repeat
        activate
    end tell
```

## Fix the Bugs

You may have already seen a potential bug in this script: What if there are no open windows?

You might assume that if someone is running this script, there will be an open window with paragraphs in it which they want numbered. This isn't a bad assumption, but if that person *does* run this script with no open windows, an error will occur. You don't want that—it makes your scripts look bad.

While that can be fixed easily enough by using the make command to create a new window, remember that the script's purpose is to number paragraphs, and a new window is empty. A further complication is that as far as AppleScript is concerned, there is a paragraph in the empty window—it just doesn't contain letters. Thus, the script will put the word "1. " at the beginning of the first line. The answer here is not to check if there is a paragraph or not, but to check if any text is present in the window. If there's no text, then there aren't any paragraphs you would want to number.

So you'll want to check a) if a window is open and b) if it has text in it. You can kill both birds with one stone by placing a conditional at the beginning of the script and using an "and" modifier to check both conditions at the same time. The resulting script looks like this:

```
(* This script numbers all the paragraphs in the first window in
Scriptable Text Editor

 It uses the make command from Scriptable Text Editor to insert the
new word *)
tell application "Scriptable Text Editor"
```

```
if (window 1 exists) and (the contents of window 1 is not "")
then
    tell window 1
        repeat with i from 1 to the number of paragraphs
        --This repeat loop numbers the paragraphs
            make word at beginning of paragraph i with data
            (i as string) & ". " --i is a number so needs to be
        coerced to a string
        end repeat
        activate
    end tell
end if
end tell
```

Because of the way the "and" modifier works, if window 1 doesn't exist, AppleScript stops evaluating the conditional before looking at the second condition. Since "and" requires that all of the conditions be true, when AppleScript sees the first condition is false, it doesn't look further. As a result, the second condition won't cause an error.

You may have also noticed that a "tell" statement has been added. The script addresses the window specifically after the conditional. If a window doesn't exist, "tell window" will cause an error. To prevent that error, you must use the "tell" statement to address the window only after you have made sure that a window exists.

## Add New Features

One way to make this script more meaningful to another user would be to provide an indicator of how far the script has progressed. With a progress bar, such as the one the Finder uses while copying, you would know exactly how many paragraphs have been numbered and how many are left to go. This would be especially useful for a long document.

Unfortunately, AppleScript doesn't provide a progress bar. The next section shows you how to use the application Progress Bar to give you a status indicator in a script. This also shows how AppleScript can work with multiple applications to create more powerful and useful scripts.

## Adding a progress bar by using another application

One of AppleScript's main features enables you to tie different applications together within a single script. Progress Bar's only purpose is to show a progress bar that you update through scripting. This enables you to show how far through a script you are. Before adding it to the window numbering script, you need to learn how it is used.

## Get the Basics Working

To see how Progress Bar works, you will write a simple script that counts from 1 to 100 using Progress Bar to show how far along the counting is. This will serve as a building block for incorporating progress bars into your own scripts.

Scriptable Text Editor is able to have many items in a window. It can contain words, paragraphs, characters, and the like. In Progress Bar, only one item is in its window: the progress bar. This progress bar has five properties: the minimum value of the progress bar, the maximum value of the progress bar, the current value of the progress bar, the caption, and the sub-caption above the progress bar (see figure 4.2).

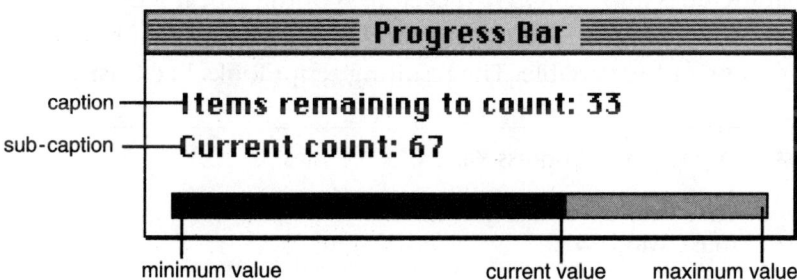

*Figure 4.2*
*The five properties of the Progress Bar.*

The first step when using Progress Bar is to set up the progress bar. When Progress Bar starts, it doesn't automatically create a new window; you must tell it to do so.

```
tell application "Progress Bar 1.0"
    activate
    make window
end tell
```

Once a new window is set up, you'll want to set the properties of the progress bar in that window. Since the script counts from 1 to 100, these are the minimum and maximum values. Adding that to the script results in:

```
tell application "Progress Bar 1.0"
    activate
    make window
    tell progress bar 1 of window 1
        set maximum value to 100
        set minimum value to 1
    end tell
end tell
```

To figure out what the current value is, the script can use a simple repeat loop which counts from 1 to 100. Because we need to know how far along the script is, we'll use a "repeat with" loop that includes a variable. With each pass of the repeat loop, the script will change the "current value" of the progress bar based on the value of the variable. The resulting script looks like this:

```
tell application "Progress Bar 1.0"
    activate
    make window
    tell progress bar 1 of window 1
```

```
        set maximum value to 100

        set minimum value to 1
            repeat with i from 1 to 100
                set current value to i
            end repeat
        end tell
    end tell
```

If you run this script, you'll see it dutifully display the progress of the count from 1 to 100. Those are the basics of using Progress Bar.

## Make It Better

Before putting a progress bar into the line numbering script, there is more that can be done to improve the look of this simple counting script.

## Improving the Progress Bar

The progress bar itself can be made more meaningful and aesthetically pleasing.

If you've been running this script through each step of its development, you may realize that you now have several windows open in Progress Bar. Progress Bar doesn't automatically close its window when it's done counting; it's up to you to do it within your script.

There are two ways to do this. You can close the window, or you can quit the application. Most of the time, you'll want to quit the application. If you're going to use a new progress bar in another part of your script, however, you may want to just close the window.

To quit the application, the script would look like this:

```
tell application "Progress Bar 1.0"
    activate
    make window
    tell progress bar 1 of window 1
        set maximum value to 100
        set minimum value to 1
        repeat with i from 1 to 100
            set current value to i
        end repeat
    end tell
    quit
end tell
```

Notice that the "quit" command is outside the inner "tell" statement. This is because the command is sent to the application, not to the progress bar window. If you want to close the window instead, use the following:

```
tell application "Progress Bar 1.0"
    activate
    make window
    tell progress bar 1 of window 1
        set maximum value to 100
        set minimum value to 1
        repeat with i from 1 to 100
            set current value to i
        end repeat
    end tell
    close window 1
end tell
```

In this case, you're telling window 1 to close. The close command comes from the Progress Bar application itself. You need to place the close command outside the second tell command because anything within the second tell command is currently being directed at the progress bar within the window, and the progress bar itself cannot be closed. In our simple counting script, there's no real purpose to closing the window—we probably won't be using the application again. It's probably easiest to just quit.

There are two more changes that will make the progress bar more informative: naming the window and giving it a caption.

By setting the name of the window, you can tell the user what process is being measured. It is useless to show the progress bar counting if you're not sure *what* it's counting. For this simple counting script, you may want to change the name to "Counting."

```
tell application "Progress Bar 1.0"
    activate
    make window
    set Name of window 1 to "Counting"
    tell progress bar 1 of window 1
        set maximum value to 100
        set minimum value to 1
        repeat with i from 1 to 100
            set current value to i
        end repeat
    end tell
    quit
end tell
```

A caption in a progress bar also gives useful information. It can tell the user exactly what is happening as it happens. Progress Bar provides you with such a caption. If you set it to "Preparing..." you tell the user that the script is doing something, but isn't counting yet. This lets the user know that something is about to happen in the progress bar.

```
tell application "Progress Bar 1.0"
    activate
    make window
    set Name of window 1 to "Counting"
    tell progress bar 1 of window 1
        set the caption to "Preparing..."
        set maximum value to 100
        set minimum value to 1
        repeat with i from 1 to 100
            set current value to i
        end repeat
    end tell
    quit
end tell
```

The caption can also be updated with new information at any point in the script. You can use the caption in this script to show what number Progress Bar is up to as it's counting (see figure 4.3). Here's how you'd do that:

```
tell application "Progress Bar 1.0"
    activate
    make window
    set Name of window 1 to "Counting"
    tell progress bar 1 of window 1
        set the caption to "Preparing..."
        set maximum value to 100
        set minimum value to 1
        repeat with i from 1 to 100
            set caption to i as string
```

```
            set current value to i
        end repeat
    end tell
    quit
end tell
```

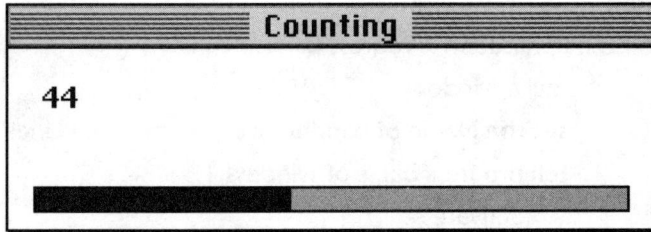

**Counting**

**44**

*Figure 4.3*
*The new and*
*improved progress*
*bar.*

## Adding a progress bar to another script

Since you already have a script that uses Progress Bar, it's easy to add a progress bar to another script. All that's required is to copy the commands from one script to the other and modify them to fit.

Look at the line-numbering script again. The first thing you want to add is the process of making the progress bar window. You have all the commands for doing this, of course, but you need to think about where they belong in the line-numbering script.

You don't want the progress bar to appear unless the script is going to run, so all those commands should be put inside the conditional. Since the repeat loop begins right after the conditional, the commands that set up the progress bar should be placed just before telling window 1 what to do. While doing this, you should change the name to something more appropriate for this script—such as "Numbering Lines." Before running the next script, you need to do a little setup. Make sure you have a window open in Scriptable Text Editor with a few paragraphs of text in it.

```
(* This script numbers all the paragraphs in the first window in
Scriptable Text Editor

 It uses the make command from Scriptable Text Editor to insert the
new word *)
tell application "Scriptable Text Editor"
    if (window 1 exists) and (the contents of window 1 is not "")
    then
        tell application "Progress Bar 1.0"
            make window
            set the Name of window 1 to "Numbering Lines"
            tell progress bar 1 of window 1
                activate
                set caption to "Preparing..."
                set maximum value to 100
                set minimum value to 1
            end tell
        end tell
        tell window 1
            repeat with i from 1 to the number of paragraphs
                --This repeat loop numbers the paragraphs
                make word at beginning of paragraph i with data
                (i as string) & ". " --i is a number so needs to be
                coerced to a string
            end repeat
            activate
        end tell
    end if
end tell
```

Simply inserting the lines from another script will not do. The
maximum value of the progress bar needs to reflect the number of
paragraphs. You only want it set to 100 if you have 100 paragraphs to number. You should set the maximum value of the

progress bar to the number of paragraphs. To do this, change the "maximum value" command to do this, as in the following script:

```
(* This script numbers all the paragraphs in the first window in
Scriptable Text Editor

 It uses the make command from Scriptable Text Editor to insert the
new word *)
tell application "Scriptable Text Editor"
    if (window 1 exists) and (the contents of window 1 is not "")
    then
        tell application "Progress Bar 1.0"
            make window
            set the Name of window 1 to "Numbering Lines"
            tell progress bar 1 of window 1
                set caption to "Preparing..."
                set maximum value to the number of paragraphs
                in window 1 of application "Scriptable Text Editor"
                set minimum value to 1
                activate
            end tell
        end tell
        tell window 1
            repeat with i from 1 to the number of paragraphs
                --This repeat loop numbers the paragraphs
                make word at beginning of paragraph i with data
                (i as string) & ". " --i is a number so needs to be
                coerced to a string
            end repeat
            activate
        end tell
    end if
end tell
```

Now that you've set up the progress bar with the maximum value equal to the number of lines in the window, all that remains is to update the progress bar as the script progresses and to close it when the script is finished. You can accomplish the update in the same repeat loop that numbers the lines. You may also want to put in a caption indicating the paragraph the script is on. The final script looks like this:

---

```
(* This script numbers all the paragraphs in the first window in
Scriptable Text Editor

  It uses the make command from Scriptable Text Editor to insert the
new word *)
tell application "Scriptable Text Editor"
    if (window 1 exists) and (the contents of window 1 is not "")
    then
        tell application "Progress Bar 1.0"
            make window
            set the Name of window 1 to "Numbering Lines"
            tell progress bar 1 of window 1
                set caption to "Preparing..."
                set maximum value to the number of paragraphs
                in window 1 of application "Scriptable Text Editor"
                set minimum value to 1
            activate
            end tell
        end tell
        tell window 1
            repeat with i from 1 to the number of paragraphs
                --This repeat loop numbers the paragraphs
                make word at beginning of paragraph i with data
                (i as string) & ". " --i is a number so needs to be
            coerced to a string
```

```
            tell application "Progress Bar 1.0"
                tell progress bar 1 of window 1
                    set current value to i
                    set caption to "Paragraph: " & (i as string)
                end tell
            end tell
        end repeat
        activate
    end tell
    tell application "Progress Bar 1.0"
        quit
    end tell
    end if
end tell
```

This script shows how easy it is to incorporate two applications into a script. Though the applications themselves are unrelated, the information from one (the number of paragraphs in the window, and the current paragraph) can be used in the other (the position of the progress bar). Using three or more programs isn't any different.

When writing scripts that use multiple applications, it helps to get parts working with individual applications and then merge them together. Just as you made a simple counting script using Progress Bar and a simple script using Scriptable Text Editor, you could create a script that takes information from a database and another script that fills in addresses in a word processor. You could then combine these two simpler scripts to make a more complex script to do a mail merge.

Combining scripts becomes easier as you build up a stock of previous scripts to draw on.

## On Your Own

At this stage you've reached the point of no return. Your journey is underway, and you're far enough down the road that you can't turn back.

Take some time to experiment before moving on to the next chapter. Try making a script with some of these elements, but based on a goal of your own.

# Chapter 5

# Building Scripts

# *Collecting Tools*

While writing a script, you may find yourself faced with a task you've dealt with before. At times like these, a library of scripts (or pieces of script) that you've already written comes in handy. You can simply insert these previously written scripts into the script you are working on.

It's best to write the library scripts with little or no dependence on the script into which they'll be placed. This makes it easier to insert them into an existing script. By copying and pasting them with little or no modification, you can save time and energy.

When writing *any* script, you should think about which parts could be added to your script library. You should also keep in mind earlier scripts you've written, from which you can copy pieces.

The text-sorting script in this section is a good example of such a script. Its function is useful in many situations, but it takes time and effort to create. By writing it once and storing it in your library, you can reuse it whenever you need it.

In addition, this script teaches a logical approach to comparisons and will further the script-writing skills you've learned so far.

## The Bubble Sort

This text-sorting script uses the "bubble sort" method—the most basic method of sorting items. It's a binary process: comparing two items, returning a true or false, then acting on that result. This sort selects a pair of items from a list, compares them and, depending on the result, changes the order of those items. This process is applied to each pair of items in succession until the entire list is sorted.

This is called a "bubble sort" because each value floats up or down through the list until it reaches its proper position.

Given the list of numbers {5, 3, 6, 4, 1} to sort from lowest to highest, the sort first finds the 5 to be higher than the 3 and exchanges their positions. The list becomes {3, 5, 6, 4, 1}. The sort continues with the second pair, 5 and 6; since they are already in their proper order, no exchange is made. This continues until the sort has compared each pair in succession. At the end of the first pass, the list looks like this:

{3, 5, 4, 1, 6}

They still are not sorted, but they are a step closer. Assuming that the numbers are completely out of order, finishing the sort would require a pass through the list once for each item except the last, since the last item is not followed by anything, and thus it has nothing to be compared to. Consequently, the list {6, 5, 4, 3, 1} would take, at most, four passes—one pass for each item minus the last.

Whenever you do a bubble sort, the number of passes required to sort a list of items is always at most equal to the number of items in the list minus one, assuming the list is completely unsorted.

## The Basics

As before, you'll write a script to control Scriptable Text Editor. For this script, you'll need some setup beforehand. Be sure Scriptable Text Editor has an open window, and type the numbers 5, 3, 6, 4, and 1 into the window with a return between each number (see figure 5.1).

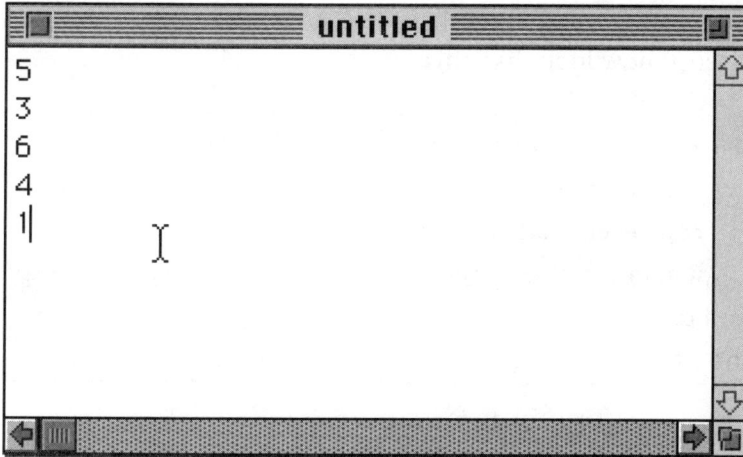

***Figure 5.1***
*Creating a
window in
Scriptable Text
Editor.*

To copy that information from Scriptable Text Editor into a
variable, "theList," you must address the application and tell it to
copy that information. So that you can see what happens while
the script runs, put the activate command into the script. Next,
put "theList" at the end of the script, so this variable will appear in
the result window at the end of each step. The script will look like
this:

```
tell window 1 of application "Scriptable Text Editor"
    activate
    copy every paragraph to theList
end tell
theList
```

The information contained in "theList" is, in fact, a list of items
where each item is a paragraph from Scriptable Text Editor.

Now that you have a list of items from Scriptable Text Editor,
you'll need a mechanism that will compare this data in pairs.
You'll use a conditional with an operator. In this case, the operator is "comes after." (For other situations, you can simply replace
this operator with another, such as: comes before, is equal to, etc.)
Don't worry about actually changing the order of the items at this

point; just tell the script to beep if they're not in the correct order. The script now looks like this:

```
tell window 1 of application "Scriptable Text Editor"
    activate
    copy every paragraph to theList
        if item 1 of theList comes after item 2 of theList then beep
    end tell
    theList
```

The above script should beep because item 1 of theList does "come after" item 2 of theList.

## Sorting Procedure

Instead of simply beeping, you want the script to exchange the positions of the numbers in the list so that they are in sorted order. To do this, copy the first item out to a temporary variable, replace the first item in the list with the second item, then place the first item back into the list in place of the second item. It's sort of a shell game—swapping the items around and exchanging their places in the list.

To achieve this you'll need a command to copy item 1 to a temporary variable:

```
tell window 1 of application "Scriptable Text Editor"
    activate
    copy every paragraph to theList
        if item 1 of theList comes after item 2 of theList then
            copy item 1 of theList to temp
        end if
    end tell
    theList
```

This copies the number you want to move. Now that item 1 is safely stored, you can replace it with item 2, as follows:

```
tell window 1 of application "Scriptable Text Editor"
    activate
    copy every paragraph to theList
    if item 1 of theList comes after item 2 of theList then
        copy item 1 of theList to temp
        set item 1 of theList to item 2 of theList
    end if
end tell
theList
```

At this point, the variable theList consists of the list {"3", "3", "6", "4", "1"}. You can see that item 1 and item 2 are the same. The next step is to set item 2 to the number you've stored in the variable "temp." This is done by setting item 2 to the number held in the variable. This will put the two items in their sorted order.

Remember that numbers from Scriptable Text Editor are treated as text, so the list will appear in the Result window with quotes around each digit.

```
tell window 1 of application "Scriptable Text Editor"
    activate
    copy every paragraph to theList
    if item 1 of theList comes after item 2 of theList then
        copy item 1 of theList to temp
        set item 1 of theList to item 2 of theList
        set item 2 of theList to temp
    end if
end tell
theList
```

## Repeated Sorting

You just created a script that does a simple bubble sort between two numbers. Because this is a bubble sort the script will need to pass through the list once for each item minus one in order for the entire list to be sorted, like so:

```
tell window 1 of application "Scriptable Text Editor"
    activate
    copy every paragraph to theList
    repeat ((the number of items in theList) - 1) times
        if item 1 of theList comes after item 2 of theList then
            copy item 1 of theList to temp
            set item 1 of theList to item 2 of theList
            set item 2 of theList to temp
        end if
    end repeat
end tell
theList
```

Repeating the script now, however, will repeatedly sort the first two numbers only; the rest will remain unsorted. The script must be told to move down the list, moving to the next pair of numbers after it has checked the first two. To do that, you'll need a variable that increments once for each pass through the list.

Every variable has to be declared. In this case, counterVar is declared in the repeat command (as a range of values between 1 and the number of items minus one). You don't need to use a "set" or "copy" command.

You can base this variable on the number of times the repeat loop has passed through the list. The repeat loop you already have in the script can use a variable, "counterVar," to count the number of times it has repeated. Item 1 of the pair becomes "item counterVar" instead of "item 1," and since item 2 of each pair is always found immediately after item 1, you can simply define it as "item (counterVar + 1)." (You need to include the parentheses to let AppleScript know that the "+ 1" applies to the variable.)

```
tell window 1 of application "Scriptable Text Editor"
    activate
    copy every paragraph to theList
```

```
        repeat with counterVar from 1 to (the number of items in
        theList) - 1
            if item counterVar of theList comes after item
            (counterVar + 1) of theList then
                copy item counterVar of theList to temp
                set item counterVar of theList to item (counterVar + 1)
                of theList
                set item (counterVar + 1) of theList to temp
            end if
        end repeat
    end tell
    theList
```

This script passes through the list once, comparing each pair of items as it goes. In doing so, it moves the highest number (6) to its proper position. The resulting list is {"3", "5", "4", "1", "6"}. The script is another step closer to being sorted. To sort it completely the script needs to repeat this process once for each item, except the last. Another repeat loop is required that will repeat the *entire* sorting process that many times.

```
    tell window 1 of application "Scriptable Text Editor"
        activate
        copy every paragraph to theList
        repeat ((the number of items in theList) - 1) times
            repeat with counterVar from 1 to (the number of items
            in theList) - 1
                if item counterVar of theList comes after item
                (counterVar + 1) of theList then
                    copy item counterVar of theList to temp
                    set item counterVar of theList to item
                    (counterVar + 1) of theList
```

```
                    set item (counterVar + 1) of theList to temp
            end if
        end repeat
    end repeat
end tell
theList
```

Finally, as you can see in the result window, you have a fully sorted list. Of course, you want it in Scriptable Text Editor's window, not the result window. To move it, you'll need to add a line to the script.

```
tell window 1 of application "Scriptable Text Editor"
    activate
    copy every paragraph to theList
    repeat ((the number of items in theList) - 1) times
        repeat with counterVar from 1 to (the number of items
        in theList) - 1
            if item counterVar of theList comes after item
            (counterVar + 1) of theList then
                copy item counterVar of theList to temp
                set item counterVar of theList to item (counterVar
                + 1) of theList
                set item (counterVar + 1) of theList to temp
            end if
        end repeat
    end repeat
    set the contents to (theList as string)
end tell
theList
```

## Cleaning Up

You can see by looking in Scriptable Text Editor's window that something is not quite right. The list was put back in as a string of numbers without returns: "13456." A sorted list in this form probably isn't much good. The script will have to insert a return between each item. You need to "traverse" the list, telling the script to insert a return for each item it comes across. In addition, the script will need to empty Scriptable Text Editor's window before placing the sorted list back into it—otherwise you would simply add this result to the original list.

To empty the window, you must set the contents to nothing.

A repeat loop is used to insert the returns in the list. With each pass through the loop, you need to concatenate the contents of the window and each item of theList in turn (using the variable currentItem), each followed by a return. While you're at it, you should remove "theList" from the end—since you are now placing the result in the window, you no longer need this command to see the results.

Before running this script, type your original unsorted list back into Scriptable Text Editor's window so it can start fresh.

```
tell window 1 of application "Scriptable Text Editor"
    activate
    copy every paragraph to theList
    repeat ((the number of items in theList) - 1) times
        repeat with counterVar from 1 to (the number of items
        in theList) - 1
            if item counterVar of theList comes after item
            (counterVar + 1) of theList then
                copy item counterVar of theList to temp
                set item counterVar of theList to item (counterVar
                + 1) of theList
                set item (counterVar + 1) of theList to temp
```

```
                    end if
                end repeat
            end repeat
            set the contents to (theList as string)
    set contents to ""
        repeat with currentItem in theList
            set the contents to the contents & currentItem & return
        end repeat
    end tell
```

This script finally does what it was intended to do. It sorts the items in the Scriptable Text Editor window and returns them to the window in the form they were taken: a list separated by returns.

Now that it functions properly, you can look for ways to make it more efficient and adaptable.

## Speeding It Up

You may have noticed that if not all the items are out of order, the script ends up doing unnecessary work. This script goes through the list as many times as there are items in that list, minus one, squared. If there are five items in the list, it goes through it four times four, or 16, times. This number is based on the fact that no matter how many items are out of order, running through the list that many times will sort the items completely.

It may be that only one number in the entire list is out of order, or it may be that no items are out of order. As it is, the script still goes through the entire sorting process. To avoid this, you can insert a mechanism at the end of each cycle of the repeat loop to check if the list is completely sorted. Then, as soon as the list is sorted, it can stop.

How will it know the list is sorted? Each time the script looks at a pair of items, it checks to see if they are in order. This check returns a true or false. If all the items return a true, then all the

items are in their proper order and the list is entirely sorted. You
need to compare how many items are in the list, minus one to the
number of items in their proper positions—that is, how many
trues are returned from the sort process. If these two numbers
match, the sort is finished and the script can stop. Here is how the
check mechanism looks, using "trueCounter" as the variable to
track the number of times the script returns a "true":

```
tell window 1 of application "Scriptable Text Editor"
    activate
    copy every paragraph to theList
    copy 0 to trueCounter
    repeat ((the number of items in theList) - 1) times
        repeat with counterVar from 1 to (the number of items
        in theList) - 1
            if item counterVar of theList comes after item
            (counterVar + 1) of theList then
                copy item counterVar of theList to temp
                set item counterVar of theList to item (counterVar
                + 1) of theList
                set item (counterVar + 1) of theList to temp
            else
                copy trueCounter + 1 to trueCounter
            end if
        end repeat
        if trueCounter is equal to ((the number of items in
        theList) - 1) then exit repeat
    end repeat
    set the contents to (theList as string)
    set contents to ""
    repeat with currentItem in theList
        set the contents to the contents & currentItem & return
    end repeat
end tell
```

Finally, you've got it running effectively and *efficiently*.

## Making it Friendly

If you like, you can give your script a bit of user-friendliness. This doesn't always mean a nice interface, as this script doesn't really need an interface at all. In fact, the best solution would be to hide it entirely. To do that, move the activate command to the end of the script, just before the "end tell," so that anyone using the script only has to see it when it has entirely finished its task.

Save this script so you can simply pull it out of your Script Library folder whenever you need a script to sort text or a list.

## On Your Own

By now you have an understanding of how you can create a larger, more advanced script. The next section deals specifically with these kinds of scripts, building fairly complex scripts piece by piece, and adding features to a script after it is up and running.

It is important to review this chapter's concepts until you feel comfortable with them before moving on.

# *Building a Boat*

The first complex script you'll write will show you how to approach the problems inherent in writing longer and more intricate scripts. You will create a utility that copies all the sounds out of a file, turning each sound into a System 7 sound file that you can play in the Finder.

## A Little Background

Sounds, as well as icons, menus, and fonts are stored in small chunks called "resources," contained within files. Since resources perform different functions, your Mac differentiates them by "type." Sounds resources are of the type 'snd ' (the space at the end is part of the name), although some programs use their own custom formats.

A file can contain any number of resources, and more than one resource in a file can be of the same type. Resources of the same type are distinguished from each other in two ways. The most common way is by ID number, which is unique within that type of resource. A resource's name also can be used to identify a resource. A resource's name, however, isn't necessarily unique, although most are to avoid confusion.

System 7 allows you to store sounds in files, called System 7 sound files, which you can access from the Finder. When you double-click a System 7 sound file the sound contained within that file is played. You can place these files into the System file itself and use them as System beeps.

## System 7 Sounds

For System 7 to play a sound, the 'snd ' resource contained within the file must have the same name as the file itself. If a sound file is named "Beep," then an 'snd ' resource contained within that file must also have the name "Beep."

The System uses two four-letter codes to distinguish different kinds of files. The first of these codes is the file's "creator," or the application that created the file. A sound file's creator is 'movr'. The second code tells the System what type of file it is. For sound files, the type is 'sfil', which stands for "sound file."

## Getting Ready to Script

For each sound in a given file, this script will create an empty System 7 sound file, extract the sound, and place it into that new file. Once you've selected a file from which to extract sounds, your first step will be to find out how many 'snd ' resources are in the file. Then, for each 'snd ' resource, create a System 7 sound file with a type of 'sfil', a creator of 'movr', and the same name as the 'snd ' resource you are placing into it.

The programs you've worked with until now don't have the capability to do this. You'll need to use two new items from the disk: ResMover and Finder Liaison.

ResMover is a scripting addition written specifically to manipulate resources. The four ResMover commands you will use for this script are "count resources," "copy resources," "get name of resource," and "set name of resource."

Finder Liaison is a utility that enables AppleScript to manipulate the Finder directly. While Finder Liaison is quite powerful, for this script you'll only use four of its commands: "create," "set type," "set creator," and "get path."

*You'll need to copy ResMover to the Scripting Additions folder found in your Extensions folder and restart your Macintosh, as AppleScript only gathers commands from scripting additions at startup.*

## Get the Basics Working

Choosing a sound file is simple. There is a file in the Tao AppleScript folder called "Tao Sounds" provided just for this script. Using this file will ensure that you get results consistent with those presented in the text. To choose this file from your script, you need to use the scripting addition Choose File. To see how it works, type the following into Script Editor and press Run:

```
choose file
```

A standard directory dialog box appears (see figure 6.1). Select "Tao Sounds" from the Tao AppleScript folder and click "Open."

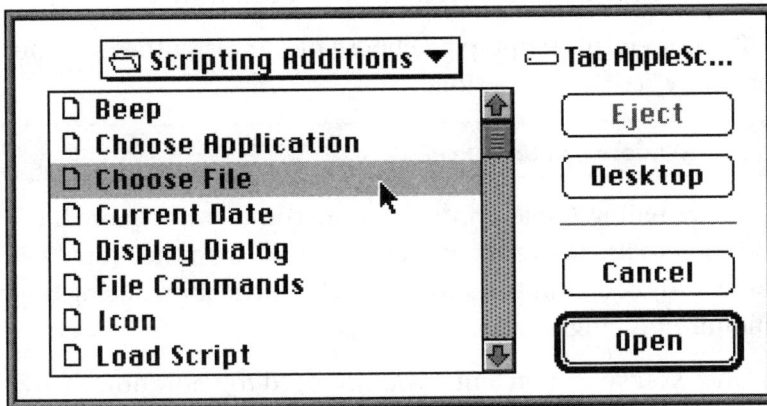

*Figure 6.1*
*A standard directory dialog box created by the Choose File command.*

The result of this script, which you can see in the result window, is a "reference" to the Tao Sounds file. This reference describes the location of Tao Sounds. Your hard drive's name is on the left side and all the folders in which your file resides are listed hierarchically after the hard drive name, separated by colons. The name of the file is the last item in this string.

The word "alias" at the beginning of the string tells AppleScript that this string isn't just a string, but is actually a reference to a particular file.

Now that you've identified your source file, you'll want to put that information into a variable so you can use it later. To do so, add a line to your script which puts the value of the result into a variable named sourceFile.

```
choose file
```
**copy the** result **to** sourceFile

## Shortening your Script

Before moving on, here is a shortcut: you can condense two lines of script into one, by putting one command in parentheses within another command. AppleScript takes the result of the command in parentheses and uses that in the outer command.

To shorten this script, put "choose file" in parentheses within the "copy" command, as follows:

**copy** (choose file) **to** sourceFile

You're telling AppleScript to run the command "choose file" and then to use the result of that command with the "copy" command. You'll find this to be a useful tactic for reducing the amount of typing you do.

To find what commands are available when using a scripting addition, you can open its dictionary with Script Editor's "Open Dictionary…" command.

Once you've chosen a file, you will need to know how many sound resources are in the file. To do this you'll use ResMover's "count resources" command. This command requires that you specify what kind of resource you're interested in and what file to look in. Your new script should look like this:

```
copy (choose file) to sourceFile
```
count resources of type "snd " in sourceFile

Run this script and choose "Tao Sounds." The result window will contain 3, the number of 'snd ' resources in that file.

Because you'll be using this number frequently, you may want to put it into a variable, as in the following script:

```
copy (choose file) to sourceFile
```
**copy** (count resources of type "snd " in sourceFile) **to** resCount

The script now puts the number of resources within that file into the variable "resCount" so you can use it later.

You now have the name of the file to pull the sounds from and the number of sounds in that file. Now you need a file to place the sound into.

When you create a file, you must first give it a name. Since the name of a System 7 sound file must match the sound resource within it, you'll first need to get the name of the resource you'll be placing in the file. This will become the name of the file itself.

ResMover can get the name of a resource if you tell it the resource's ID or the relative position of the resource within the file. The position of a resource is determined by its ID number relative to those of other resources found within that file. That is, if a series of resources have IDs of 549, 6, and 2684, they would be referred to as resource 2, resource 1, and resource 3 respectively; the lowest ID number is first, and the highest ID number is last.

You can use the shortcut you learned earlier to put the result of the "get name of resource" command into the variable named "resName." Doing so gives you the following:

```
copy (choose file) to sourceFile

copy (count resources of type "snd " in sourceFile) to resCount

copy (get name of resource number 1 of type "snd " in
sourceFile) to resName
```

The result window now shows the name of the first 'snd ' resource in "Tao Sounds."

With this information, you can create a file to hold the re-source. To create the actual file, you must use Finder Liaison's "create" command, which creates a blank file at the location you specify.

Specifying a file's location with Finder Liaison is different from the reference that "choose file" returned—which ResMover uses. Instead of "Thendara:Sounds:Beep" to refer to the file "beep", whose location is on a hard drive named "Thendara," in a folder named "sounds", Finder Liaison uses a phrase such as "file 'Beep' in folder 'Sounds' in disk 'Thendara'."

To "create," you need to name the file and tell Finder Liaison where to put it. To ensure the file and the resource within it have the same name, you can use the information stored in resName and the name of the resource, to name the new file.

There's still one more complication to consider: Finder Liaison will generate an error if you attempt to create a file that already exists. Because you'll be running this script several times, you'll will need to either override this "alert" or delete the file you just made each time you run the script. You can override the alert in Finder Liaison from within your script. To do so you must use the "replace" parameter and follow it with the word "yes" or "no" to indicate whether Finder Liaison should replace the file if it already exists. Since you will only be losing a sound file, you should allow Finder Liaison to overwrite an existing file.

Once you've created the file, you need to turn it into a System 7 sound file by assigning it the appropriate type and creator. Finder Liaison's "set type of" and "set creator of," commands can set these type and creator codes. Remembering to use Finder Liaison's method of pointing to files, you can add these commands to your script, like so:

> In these example scripts the hard disk "Thendara" is used. This is the name of Derrick's hard disk. You should use the name of your own hard disk. You'll also need to create a folder named "Sounds" at the root level of your hard disk.

```
copy (choose file) to sourceFile

copy (count resources of type "snd " in sourceFile) to resCount

copy (get name of resource number 1 of type "snd " in sourceFile) to resName

tell application "Finder Liaison 1.0"

    Create File resName in Folder "Sounds" in Disk "Thendara"
    replacing yes
```

```
        Set Type of File resName in Folder "Sounds" in Disk
        "Thendara" to "sfil"

        Set Creator of File resName in Folder "Sounds" in Disk
        "Thendara" to "movr"
end tell
```

After you run this script, go to the Finder and you'll see that
your folder has a new System 7 sound (see figure 6.2).

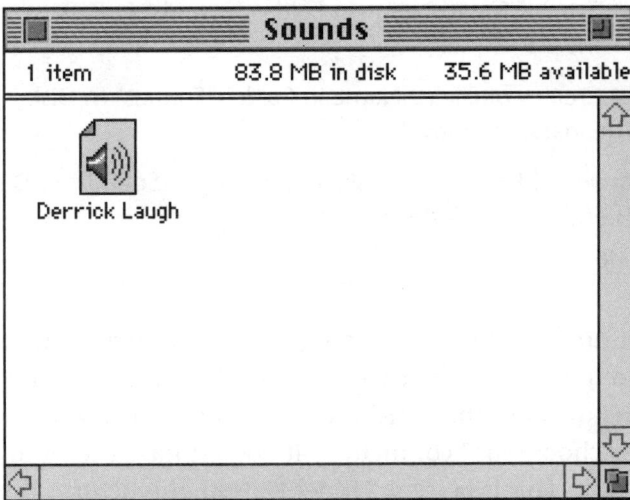

*Figure 6.2*
*A System 7 sound
file in the sounds
folder, created by
your script.*

There's one last step before copying the 'snd ' resource to this
new file. When you work with ResMover, you must specify files
using the references you learned earlier. Though you know the
name of the file, you must still give ResMover the full path of the
file.

To facilitate working with other programs, Finder Liaison has
the command "Get Path of" which, given a path to a file that it
recognizes, returns a string that points to the file in the format
ResMover recognizes. To get the path of your destination file, use
this command and store the result in a variable named destFile:

```
copy (choose file) to sourceFile

copy (count resources of type "snd " in sourceFile) to resCount

copy (get name of resource number 1 of type "snd " in sourceFile)
to resName

tell application "Finder Liaison 1.0"

    Create File resName in Folder "Sounds" in Disk "Thendara"
    replacing yes

    Set Type of File resName in Folder "Sounds" in Disk
    "Thendara" to "sfil"

    Set Creator of File resName in Folder "Sounds" in Disk
    "Thendara" to "movr"

    copy (Get Path of File resName in Folder "Sounds" in Disk
    "Thendara") to destFile

end tell
```

When running this script, you'll see that the result window will contain a reference string that points to the file. However, you'll notice that it is not the same as the earlier reference when you used the "choose file" command—it doesn't have the word "alias" in front of it. This is because Finder Liaison only returns the string; you must tell AppleScript to interpret this string as a file reference. When you do this, you use the word "file" instead of "alias." You'll need to know this in the next step, when you'll be using the string to reference a file. Here's an example:

```
file destFile
```

Now that you've created a file to draw sounds from and established a way to make a new file for each of those sounds, you need only copy each sound from the original file to its new file.

ResMover has a "copy resource" command that enables you to copy a resource from one file to another. You can tell it which resource, of a given type, to use by specifying it by name, ID number, or index—just as you could with "get name of resource." Here's what the resulting script looks like:

```
copy (choose file) to sourceFile

copy (count resources of type "snd " in sourceFile) to resCount

copy (get name of resource number 1 of type "snd " in sourceFile)
to resName

tell application "Finder Liaison 1.0"

    Create File resName in Folder "Sounds" in Disk "Thendara"
    replacing yes

    Set Type of File resName in Folder "Sounds" in Disk
    "Thendara" to "sfil"

    Set Creator of File resName in Folder "Sounds" in Disk
    "Thendara" to "movr"

    copy (Get Path of File resName in Folder "Sounds" in Disk
    "Thendara") to destFile

end tell
```

```
copy resource number 1 of type "snd " from sourceFile to file
destFile
```

Notice that you must precede destFile with the word "file." This isn't necessary with sourceFile, as it is already included in the value of the variable.

When you run this script, it will extract the first sound from the file "Tao Sounds" and place it into a newly created System 7 sound file.

Having learned how to extract a single sound, it's time to give the script the capability to extract multiple sounds. You'll need a repeat loop to count from 1 to the number of "snd " resources found in the file. You already have a variable equal to the number of resources in a given file: the "resCount" variable.

The repeat loop will contain a counter variable named "counter," and instead of having the script extract 'snd' resource number 1, you'll tell it to extract the 'snd' resource with the number equal to the variable "counter."

```
copy (choose file) to sourceFile

copy (count resources of type "snd " in sourceFile) to resCount

repeat with counter from 1 to resCount

    copy (get name of resource number counter of type "snd " in
    sourceFile) to resName

    tell application "Finder Liaison 1.0"

        Create File resName in Folder "Sounds" in Disk "Thendara"
        replacing yes

        Set Type of File resName in Folder "Sounds" in Disk
        "Thendara" to "sfil"

        Set Creator of File resName in Folder "Sounds" in Disk
        "Thendara" to "movr"

        copy (Get Path of File resName in Folder "Sounds" in Disk
        "Thendara") to destFile

    end tell

    copy resource number counter of type "snd " from sourceFile
    to file destFile

end repeat
```

What happens when there are no 'snd ' resources in the file you selected? ResMover, when asked how many 'snd ' resources are found within a file with no 'snd ' resources, will return a zero; the repeat loop won't run, and the script will exit. If the final number of a repeat loop is lower than the initial number (unless you use "by" to count backwards), the repeat loop will not run.

Run this script, and choose "Tao Sounds." When the script is finished, you'll have three System 7 sound files in your folder. You now have a "first draft" of Sound Sucker!

## Make It Better

Now that you have a Sound Sucker script, you should take some time to find ways of improving it. One way would be to add the capabilities of Progress Bar.

With a progress bar, you will know how far along the script is for a given file. You already have a script that provides a progress bar, so you can simply transfer the necessary lines of that script into this new script.

You already have the maximum value for the progress bar: the total number of 'snd' resources in the file, stored in the variable resCount. You can place the first part of your progress bar script at the beginning, after placing values into resCount and resName.

You can, of course, put the part that increments the progress bar anywhere within the repeat loop. Remember, however, that you'd like to make the progress bar an accurate portrayal of what's going on. To make the progress bar as informative as possible, you also may want to set the caption to the name of the sound currently being manipulated.

So far in this book, you've updated the progress bar's caption and current value at the same time. This approach doesn't work well for this particular script. If those commands are put at the beginning of the repeat loop, then the progress bar will be incremented before the sound has been moved. If they are put at the end of the repeat loop, the progress bar will be incremented, but the name of the sound that has already been moved will still be in the caption.

To make the information in the progress bar accurate, you must update the caption at the beginning of the repeat loop and the progress bar at the end.

Here's another shortcut. To update just the caption of the progress bar, you may expect to type something like this:

```
tell window 1 of application "Progress Bar 1.0"
    set the caption of progress bar 1 to "Extracting"
end tell
```

This may seem like a great deal of text to execute only one command. However, AppleScript enables you to use the "tell" command to send a single command to an application on one line. Using this capability, setting the caption would look like this:

```
tell window 1 of application "Progress Bar 1.0" to set the
caption of progress bar 1 to "Extracting" & resName
```

This will put something like "Extracting Derrick Laugh" in the progress bar window. You also can use this technique to set the current value of the progress bar, at the end of the repeat loop:

```
tell window 1 of application "Progress Bar 1.0" to set the
current value of progress bar 1 to counter
```

This last command uses the variable "counter" as the current value of the progress bar. This makes sense, since counter represents the number of times you've passed through the repeat loop.

The last step is to quit the two applications the script has been working with. This must be done after the "end repeat" so that the programs will quit only when the script has completed extracting the sounds from the chosen file. Adding these steps, your final script looks like this:

```
copy (choose file) to sourceFile

copy (count resources of type "snd " in sourceFile) to resCount

tell application "Progress Bar 1.0"
    make window
    tell window 1
        set the Name to "Sound Sucker"
```

```
            set the minimum value of progress bar 1 to 1

            set the maximum value of progress bar 1 to resCount

            set the caption of progress bar 1 to "Preparing..."

            activate

        end tell

    end tell

    repeat with counter from 1 to resCount

        copy (get name of resource number counter of type "snd " in
        sourceFile) to resName

        tell window 1 of application "Progress Bar 1.0" to set the
        caption of progress bar 1 to "Extracting:" & resName

        tell application "Finder Liaison 1.0"

            Create File resName in Folder "Sounds" in Disk "Thendara"
            replacing yes

            Set Type of File resName in Folder "Sounds" in Disk
            "Thendara" to "sfil"

            Set Creator of File resName in Folder "Sounds" in Disk
            "Thendara" to "movr"

            copy (Get Path of File resName in Folder "Sounds" in Disk
            "Thendara") to destFile

        end tell

        copy resource number counter of type "snd " from sourceFile
        to file destFile

        tell window 1 of application "Progress Bar 1.0" to set the
        current value of progress bar 1 to counter

    end repeat

    tell application "Finder Liaison 1.0" to quit

    tell application "Progress Bar 1.0" to quit
```

You can now run this script, choose a file, and get a progress bar indicating how far along it is. When the script has finished, the two applications used will quit, and you'll have the sounds you wanted, all ready to be double-clicked and played from within the Finder.

## Fix the Bugs

There are always bugs to be fixed before the script will run as expected.

The first bug arises if an 'snd ' resource doesn't have a name. Remember that naming resources is optional. If one of the sounds in a file does not have a name, ResMover will return an empty string. When Finder Liaison tries to create a file with no name, it generates an error because the System does not allow a file without a name.

To avoid this, you must determine if an 'snd' resource without a name is present. Each resource's name is stored in the variable resName, so a conditional can be created to check the value of resName before that value is used to create and work with a sound file.

---

**if** resName = "" **then** beep

---

On the third line of the script, resName is defined. This conditional should be placed directly after the variable is declared, so that if there is a problem it can be addressed immediately.

If the conditional does beep, what should you do? You could change the name of the resource right in the source file, but you should never change an original file.

It's only important that the resource and file have the same name when the sound is played, so you can simply make a file with a generic name, move the resource into the file, and then assign the resource that generic name.

A good way to name generic files is to number them—as the Finder does with untitled items. The first unnamed resource would be placed in the file "No Name 1," the second in "No Name 2," etc. This way, each unnamed resource will be placed into a uniquely named file.

To do this, you must create a variable that will be incremented each time an unnamed resource is encountered. When the original resource has no name, this variable will be used to put a value into resName along with the generic name. You should remember that if the resource has a name this conditional will not run and the name of the original resource name will be transferred as usual.

Before using this new counting variable, you need to declare it. In general, it's a good idea to declare any variables at the beginning of a script so that the variable will be available for use.

Declare a variable named "unnamedCounter" at the beginning of the script and give it an initial value of 1, as follows:

```
copy 1 to unnamedCounter
```

Within the conditional, you'll need to place a new value into resName and increment the value of unnamedCounter. You've already seen how to do these things, so remove "beep," insert these commands, and place an "end if" after them. The new conditional looks like this:

```
if resName is "" then
    copy "No Name " & unnamedCounter to resName
    copy unnamedCounter + 1 to unnamedCounter
end if
```

You haven't actually changed the name of the resource, only the value of resName. The script will move the resource into the sound file it creates, but the sound will not play because the names of the resource and the file do not yet match.

Once the resource has been copied to its new location, you can set its name. ResMover provides the command "set name of resource" for this purpose. You must first provide it with some information.

You must tell it which resource to change. As there is only one resource in the sound file just created, it can simply be referred to as resource number 1. You must tell it the type of the resource: 'snd '. You also need to specify the file what file contains this particular resource. This information is in the variable destFile. Finally, you need to tell resMover what to name the resource. This name is stored in the variable resName. Here's what the final command looks like:

```
set name of resource number 1 of type "snd " in file destFile to
resName
```

You should place this directly after the command that copies the resource into the new file. If it is placed earlier, the resource won't have been copied into the file yet.

## Complications

What happens when there are no sound resources to move? You may remember that this wasn't going to be a problem, because the repeat loop would do nothing if it was counting from a higher number to a lower number. But, that was before a progress bar was added.

As the script now stands, it will first set up a progress bar and then quit the application. While this isn't exactly a bug, the result is certainly unattractive.

Fortunately, the solution is simple. Place the segment of the script that sets up the progress bar into a conditional. This conditional will execute the commands within it only if there are more than zero sound resources in the selected file.

This solves the progress bar problem, but what happens at the end of the script? When AppleScript attempts to quit the applications, it launches each one, only to quit each one as soon as it is launched. Again, you must enclose these commands in a conditional so that they will be executed only when there are more than zero sound resources. The programs will be launched only if there are resources that need to be dealt with. Enclosing the commands results in this final script:

```
copy (choose file) to sourceFile
copy 1 to unnamedCounter
copy (count resources of type "snd " in sourceFile) to resCount
if (count resources of type "snd " in sourceFile) > 0 then
    tell application "Progress Bar 1.0"
        make window
        tell window 1
            set the Name to "Sound Sucker"
            set the minimum value of progress
            bar 1 to 1
            set the maximum value of progress bar 1
            to resCount
            set the caption of progress bar 1 to "Pre-
            paring..."
            activate
        end tell
    end tell
end if
repeat with counter from 1 to resCount
    copy (get name of resource number counter of type "snd "
    in sourceFile) to resName
    if resName is "" then
        copy "No Name " & unnamedCounter to resName
        copy unnamedCounter + 1 to unnamedCounter
    end if
```

```
tell window 1 of application "Progress Bar 1.0" to set the
caption of progress bar 1 to "Extracting:" & resName

tell application "Finder Liaison 1.0"

    Create File resName in Folder "Sounds" in Disk
    "Thendara" replacing yes

    Set Type of File resName in Folder "Sounds" in
    Disk "Thendara" to "sfil"

    Set Creator of File resName in Folder "Sounds" in
    Disk "Thendara" to "movr"

    copy (Get Path of File resName in Folder "Sounds"
    in Disk "Thendara") to destFile

end tell

copy resource number counter of type "snd " from
sourceFile to file destFile

set name of resource number 1 of type "snd " in file
destFile to resName

tell window 1 of application "Progress Bar 1.0" to set the
current value of progress bar 1 to counter

end repeat

if (count resources of type "snd " in sourceFile) > 0 then

    tell application "Finder Liaison 1.0" to quit

    tell application "Progress Bar 1.0" to quit

end if
```

## Continuing On

Remember that sounds contained in commercial or shareware applications are the property of the authors.

Now that you have a script that works well, play with it! Suck sounds! Get sounds from games, stacks, anything. And, when you get tired of it, move on to the next chapter to find out how to make your script into an easy to use stand-alone application for your sound sucking needs.

# *Going Downstream*

This chapter shows you how to turn Sound Sucker into a stand-alone script that performs just like a "real" application. This script also results in a fun little utility, that *you* wrote.

You can run a stand-alone script (or "script application") just like any application, by double-clicking on the icon in the Finder to launch the script. You won't need to use Script Editor to run the script, but you must have AppleScript installed. This is a very useful way of distributing scripts. By making a script into an application, you avoid forcing others to use Script Editor; it only matters whether AppleScript is installed and that the additions and applications used in the script are available.

AppleScript can create two kinds of script applications. The first is a simple stand-alone application, that, when its icon is double-clicked, opens a dialog box with the options of running the script or quitting.

The second kind of application allows drag-and-drop capabilities. Drag-and-drop applications are a feature of System 7. When files are dragged onto the icon of an application, that application performs certain commands on those files. For example, when you drag and drop script applications onto the icon of Script Editor, it opens them as scripts—as opposed to running them as applications when you double-click on them. You also can drag the icon of an application onto Script Editor and it will open the application's dictionary, if it has one.

Although you'll create these two types of script applications, with Sound Sucker you'll use the drag-and-drop type, since it's more useful for a utility that affects other files, as this one does. By the end of this section, you'll be able to drag a whole range of files onto a Sound Sucker icon and have it extract all the sounds from the files.

## Saving as a Script Application

It's a snap creating a script application from a script. You simply save it as an application. To see an example of this, use the "Save As..." command from the File menu in Script Editor. You'll get a typical Save dialog box except that, under the area where you type in the name of the file, you'll see a pop-up menu (see figure 7.1). This menu contains all your saving options—one of which is to save the script as an application.

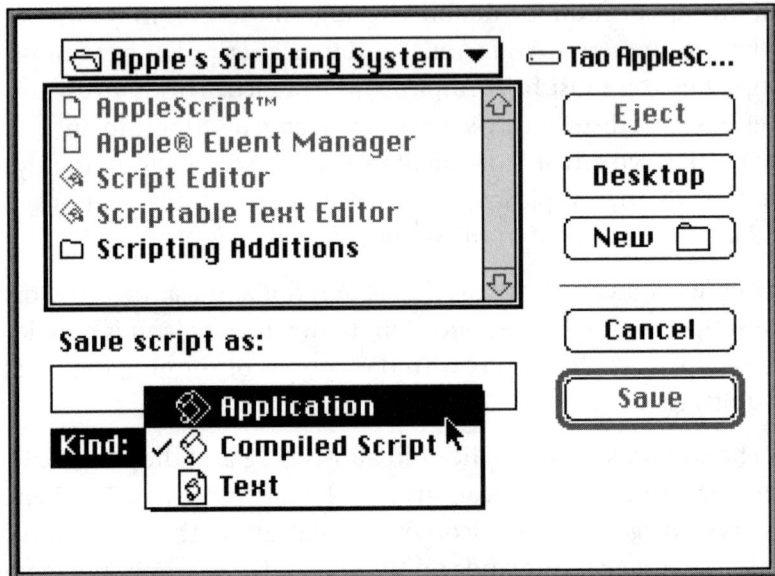

*Figure 7.1*
*Saving your script
as a script
application.*

Once you select the "Application" option, you'll see two check boxes. The first one enables you to keep the script application running after it has finished. (Normally, a script application quits once the script within finishes, but because it is possible to have a script that performs commands after a particular event occurs, this is an important option.)

The second option enables you to skip the splash screen that appears when you launch the script. With the splash screen, the user has to specifically tell the script to run after double-clicking on its icon. This prevents running a script accidentally. Turning this option on makes the script application simply run when it is opened, without asking for confirmation.

For the moment, don't worry about these check boxes. Leave them unchecked, and save your script.

To run the script application, you must close the window of the script in Script Editor. If you leave the script open in Script Editor when you try to run the application you'll receive an error.

Once you've closed the window, go back to the Finder and launch the script application you've just made. You'll get a splash screen and, when you press Run, the script will run.

## Adding Drop-ability

Now you can make a stand-alone application, but if you drag some files onto the icon of the script application it won't do anything. Making a script application with this drag-and-drop capability (commonly known as a "droplet") requires that you make some changes to the script contained in it.

When you drag a set of icons onto a script application, with drag-and-drop capability, a message is sent to the application that contains a list of all the files that were dropped onto the application. AppleScript can intercept this message and, upon receiving it, run a script.

The message that is sent is "open." To intercept it, you write "on open," as in the following:

```
on open
    beep
end open
```

This script will beep when you drag a set of files onto it. You must limit which commands operate on the opened files by writing "end open."

However, there's more to the message than the message itself. As you learned earlier, the script application gets a list of all files dragged onto it. This list should be placed into an "argument," a value that the script needs before it can run. To place this list into an argument, you use a variable.

You define the variable in which to place the argument as part of the "on open" statement by enclosing the name of the variable in parentheses immediately after the statement, as in:

```
on open (docList)
    beep
end open
```

When files are dragged onto this script application, AppleScript sets the value of docList to a list in which each item is a reference to a file.

You can add these two commands to the Sound Sucker script, enclosing the entire script in those two statements. You still must deal with the information in the docList variable, however, and incorporate it into your script.

## Adding to Sound Sucker

You no longer need to pick a file to suck sounds from at the beginning of the script. You can select the files by dragging them onto the icon. Because of this, you can remove the first line of the script.

Since you want to run this script once for every value in docList, you can use a repeat loop to traverse the list, as you did in the "sorting" script. The variable sourceFile that you use in the script can be used as the counting variable for the repeat loop, so you don't need to change that aspect of the script. It now looks like this:

```
on open (docList)
    copy 1 to unnamedCounter
    repeat with sourceFile in docList
        copy (count resources of type "snd " in sourceFile) to
        resCount
        if (count resources of type "snd " in sourceFile) > 0 then
            tell application "Progress Bar 1.0"
                make window
                tell window 1
                    set the Name to "Sound Sucker"
                    set the minimum value of progress bar 1 to 1
                    set the maximum value of progress bar 1 to
                    resCount
                    set the caption of progress bar 1 to
                    "Preparing..."
                    activate
                end tell
            end tell
        end if
        repeat with counter from 1 to resCount
            copy (get name of resource number counter of type
            "snd " in sourceFile) to resName
            if resName is "" then
                copy "No Name " & unnamedCounter to
                resName
                copy unnamedCounter + 1 to unnamedCounter
            end if
```

```
            tell window 1 of application "Progress Bar 1.0" to set
            the caption of progress bar 1 to "Extracting:" &
            resName
            tell application "Finder Liaison 1.0"
                Create File resName in Folder "Sounds" in Disk
                "Thendara" replacing yes
                Set Type of File resName in Folder "Sounds" in
                Disk "Thendara" to "sfil"
                Set Creator of File resName in Folder "Sounds" in
                Disk "Thendara" to "movr"
                copy (Get Path of File resName in Folder "Sounds"
                in Disk "Thendara") to destFile
            end tell
            copy resource number counter of type "snd " from
            sourceFile to file destFile
            set name of resource number 1 of type "snd " in file
            destFile to resName
            tell window 1 of application "Progress Bar" to set the
            current value of progress bar 1 to counter
        end repeat
    end repeat
    if (count resources of type "snd " in sourceFile) > 0 then
        tell application "Finder Liaison 1.0" to quit
        tell application "Progress Bar 1.0" to quit
    end if
end open
```

You'll notice that the repeat loop ended before the applications quit. This is because you want the applications to quit only after you're finished with them. This raises an interesting problem.

## Fixing Bugs

If you run this script with more than just a few files, Progress Bar will soon return an "Out of Memory" error. This is because you've made a new window every time you went through the new repeat

loop. To fix this, you can add a command to close Progress Bar's
window at the end of the repeat loop.

```
on open (docList)
    copy 1 to unnamedCounter
    repeat with sourceFile in docList
        copy (count resources of type "snd " in sourceFile) to
        resCount
        if (count resources of type "snd " in sourceFile) > 0 then
            tell application "Progress Bar 1.0"
                make window
                tell window 1
                    set the Name to "Sound Sucker"
                    set the minimum value of progress bar 1 to 1
                    set the maximum value of progress bar 1 to
                    resCount
                    set the caption of progress bar 1 to "Prepar-
                    ing..."
                    activate
                end tell
            end tell
        end if
        repeat with counter from 1 to resCount
            copy (get name of resource number counter of type
            "snd " in sourceFile) to resName
            if resName is "" then
                copy "No Name " & unnamedCounter to resName
                copy unnamedCounter + 1 to unnamedCounter
            end if
            tell window 1 of application "Progress Bar 1.0" to set
            the caption of progress bar 1 to "Extracting:" &
            resName
            tell application "Finder Liaison 1.0"
```

```
            Create File resName in Folder "Sounds" in Disk
            "Thendara" replacing yes
            Set Type of File resName in Folder "Sounds" in
            Disk "Thendara" to "sfil"
            Set Creator of File resName in Folder "Sounds" in
            Disk "Thendara" to "movr"
            copy (Get Path of File resName in Folder "Sounds"
            in Disk "Thendara") to destFile
        end tell
        copy resource number counter of type "snd " from
        sourceFile to file destFile
        set name of resource number 1 of type "snd " in file
        destFile to resName
        tell window 1 of application "Progress Bar 1.0" to set
        the current value of progress bar 1 to counter
    end repeat
        tell application "Progress Bar 1.0" to close window 1
    end repeat
    if (count resources of type "snd " in sourceFile) > 0 then
        tell application "Finder Liaison 1.0" to quit
        tell application "Progress Bar 1.0" to quit
    end if
end open
```

This is the final Sound Sucker script. You can now save it as a script application. You'll notice that the icon for the application in the AppleScript pop-up menu has a small arrow. AppleScript recognizes that you are making this script into a droplet because of the script command that intercepts the "open" message. The option for keeping the application open should be left unchecked as you probably will want to quit it when it is finished. You need not be concerned about the splash screen as it won't appear unless you specifically double-click on the application. Click Save!

You now have a stand-alone utility that you can use as long as you have AppleScript, ResMover, and Progress Bar installed on your machine. Simply drag files onto it and AppleScript will extract all the "snd " resources from them. This is a great way for getting new beep sounds. You can then drag these sound files onto the System Folder and they will be automatically installed into your System.

## One Last Thing

If you're going to drag applications with a lot of sounds in them onto this script's icon, you may want to increase the amount of memory allotted to the script application. To do this, select its icon, choose "Get Info" from the File menu, and increase the number in the preferred size field (you might start by doubling it).

## On Your Own

Take some time to make your own droplets and script applications. They can be fun and useful. Try changing the sorting script so that you can simply drag a Scriptable Text Editor document onto it and sort all the lines. The possibilities are endless. You have the power to make your own custom utilities and tools that are as easy to use as any Macintosh application.

# Chapter 8

# Complex Scripts

# *Climbing the Mountain*

In this section, you'll create an application that can find and replace text in filenames in the Finder. This script is fairly long and goes through many steps on the way to its final stage, but the result is a truly amazing and useful script.

You will create a script that can search a hard drive, and also the interface for getting the criteria by which you will search and replace.

## Directory Traversal Using AppleScript's Messages

In the previous section, you learned that a script can intercept messages from the System and that script commands can be attached to those messages, so that certain actions can be carried out when that message is interpreted. AppleScript also enables you to have a script send messages, and to have another part of the script intercept these messages.

For this script, you will learn to use "directory traversals." A directory traversal searches through each item in a hard drive or folder and performs a specific action on each item. If there is a folder within that drive or folder, the script will look at all the items within it as well. This process continues until all the folders have been run through. This is similar to traversing a list with a repeat loop, which runs commands once for each item in a list.

This capability is very powerful, as you don't need to specify by name which files you will affect. You can choose any set of files, including all the files on your hard drive or only those which meet certain criteria.

Your first use of directory traversals will be to remove the text " alias" from alias filenames anywhere on your hard drive. You don't need to be told a file is an alias; its name is always italicized. (The space before "alias" is also part of the text to be deleted.) You'll then move on to true find-and-replace capability, incorporating dialog boxes into the script's interface.

## Handling Messages

The first step is learning to work with messages and subroutines.

You learned to intercept a message when you intercepted the System's "open" command in the Sound Sucker script. Sending and intercepting a message from within a script works the same way. You simply write:

```
message1()
```

When you run this script, the script receives a message that tells it to run the set of commands (the "subroutine") called "message1." AppleScript then searches the script for a "subroutine" with that name.

A subroutine in AppleScript is a set of commands located from within a script, but isolated from it. A subroutine can be executed only when called by name in the main part of the script. By sending a message to run a subroutine you can use a specified set of commands repeatedly in your script by simply referencing them with a single command.

When your script receives this message it "calls" the named subroutine. The script then executes the commands within that subroutine. Afterward, execution picks up from the next line after the message.

If you run the above line of script, you will get an error because AppleScript won't find a subroutine with this name. You need to create one. Type the following subroutine at the end of the script (it can go anywhere, but it's customary to place a subroutine at the end of a script):

```
on message1()
    beep
end message1
```

This subroutine specifies that each time the script sends itself the message "message1," the commands within the subroutine (in this case, the command "beep") will be sent to the System.

In the Sound Sucker script, the "open" message sent information along with the message itself. This can be done with messages within the script as well. You can enclose the name of a variable within the parentheses after the message name, and the value of that variable will be sent along with the message. You may want to send or intercept several variables at once. Simply write multiple variable names within the parentheses, separated by commas, such as:

```
on message1(x, y)
    beep
end message1
```

The variables x and y are set to the value of the corresponding variables sent with the message.

They can contain any information AppleScript understands. To send a "message1" command, setting x to 3 and y to 4, you would use this command:

```
message1(3, 4)
```

You may want to have some information returned from the subroutine as well as send it. You can do this with the "return" command. Type "return" followed by the information you wish sent back to the script. This command tells the script to leave the subroutine, so when this command is executed, no further commands in the subroutine are performed.

To see this in an example, you will write a subroutine that takes a list of numbers and returns the average. The first step is to write a subroutine called "average."

```
on average( )
    beep
end average
```

To run this subroutine, send the message "average" from the main script:

```
average( )
on average( )
    beep
end average
```

An argument is the information sent to a subroutine for the subroutine to act upon.

You must provide the subroutine with a list of numbers to be averaged. You also need to designate a variable in the subroutine that can hold the list of numbers once it gets there. This variable is a parameter of the incoming message. Use the variable "listofNums" to hold the argument:

```
on average(listofNums)
    beep
end average
```

The command in the main script must be modified to send the actual list:

```
average ({1, 2, 3, 4})
```

To average the list of numbers, you must divide their sum by the number of items in the list. The script will look like this:

```
average({1, 2, 3, 4})
on average(listofNums)
    copy 0 to total
    repeat with currentNumber in listofNums
        copy currentNumber + total to total
    end repeat
    total ÷ (the number of items in listofNums)
end average
```

For this subroutine to be useful, you'll need to get information back from the subroutine. You must use the "return" command, as follows:

```
average({1, 2, 3, 4})
on average(listofNums)
    copy 0 to total
    repeat with currentNumber in listofNums
        copy currentNumber + total to total
    end repeat
    return total ÷ (the number of items in listofNums)
end average
```

While this subroutine is short, it demonstrates each of the major concepts.

Next, you will learn how to apply these concepts to a fairly complex task, using directory traversal.

THE TAO OF APPLESCRIPT

## Back to the Script

Before writing this script, you will need to explore the basic concepts behind it. This script uses Finder Liaison, introduced in the last chapter, for the file and folder searching. Finder Liaison has a command that gets the names of all the files in a given folder, and another command that gets the names of all the folders in a given folder. Finder Liaison also has a command that renames a particular file or folder.

Given the path to a folder, in a format Finder Liaison understands, the subroutine will look at all the files in that folder and rename them if any of the file names are aliases and end with "alias." When finished, the script will look in all the folders within that folder. For each folder, the script will send a message that will call the same subroutine, running those commands on the files in each folder. When complete, the script will have removed the text "alias" from the filenames of all aliases on your hard drive.

## Get the Basics Working

First, you will write the subroutine to rename aliases. The name of a subroutine follows the same rules as the name of a variable; you can use virtually anything. Here's how to start:

```
on fileWalker(currentFolder)
end fileWalker
```

A subroutine is useless unless it is called, so you'll need to add lines to the main script to call it.

The path of the file or folder to be searched must be sent to the subroutine.

AppleScript provides a mechanism that generates this path. Putting the phrase "a reference to" in front of a path to an object tells a subroutine to use the object path rather than the value of the object itself.

Set a reference to your own hard drive (rather than Thendara) in the main script and place that reference into the variable "folderName." You'll need to do this with Finder Liaison.

```
tell application "Finder Liaison 1.0"
    copy (a reference to Disk "Thendara") to folderName
end tell
```

```
on fileWalker(currentFolder)
end fileWalker
```

When you run this script, the result window contains the path to the object you specified. This path is stored in the variable folderName.

By the way, it's convenient to separate subroutines from the main script by an extra line space, as above.

## Getting the Message Across

Now that you've put the reference into a variable, you want to give that information to the fileWalker subroutine. You can do this by calling it as you would any subroutine:

```
tell application "Finder Liaison 1.0"
    copy (a reference to Disk "Thendara") to folderName
end tell
fileWalker(folderName)
```

```
on fileWalker(currentFolder)
end fileWalker
```

You may wonder why you place all of these commands on separate lines. Why can't you write "fileWalker (a reference to Disk 'Thendara' of application 'Finder Liaison')?" This an instance where the "tell" command isn't a shortcut—it's necessary. When you use the "tell" command, AppleScript looks at the application you specify and reads in all the information about the commands and objects which that application understands. Using "window 1," is no problem, as AppleScript knows what a window object is, but it doesn't know what a "Disk" object is.

In order for the script to compile, you must refer to Finder Liaison with a "tell" command. AppleScript will then read in the information and be able to understand a "Disk" object.

So why can't you write "fileWalker (a reference to Disk 'Thendara')" inside a tell statement? When you send a message from within a tell statement, AppleScript attempts to send that message to the application rather than back to the script itself. This generates an error.

Now that you've successfully sent a path to the subroutine fileWalker, what do you do with it?

## First Work with the Files

You can get a list of all the files in a particular folder by using Finder Liaison's "Get Files in" command, as follows:

```
tell application "Finder Liaison 1.0"
    copy (a reference to Disk "Thendara") to folderName
end tell
fileWalker(folderName)


on fileWalker(currentFolder)
    tell application "Finder Liaison 1.0"
        Get Files in currentFolder
    end tell
end fileWalker
```

When you run this script, you'll get a list of all the files on the top level of your hard drive. Even if you only have folders on the top level, you still will get some items in the list, as there are two invisible Desktop files and perhaps other invisible files located here.

The next step will determine if any of these files end with " alias" so that they can be removed. While it would be better to do this only if the file is an alias, there's no way for AppleScript to determine whether a file is an alias or not. (This is addressed below.) For now, make an alias of some application and put it on the top level of your hard drive. Make sure that the file doesn't end up with the same name as another item on the top level of your hard drive once " alias" is removed, as the Macintosh won't allow two items in the same level to have the same name. This will be addessed soon as well.

Since the names of all the files are in a list, each one can be looked at individually by traversing the list with a repeat loop (using "beep" as a temporary "dummy" command):

```
tell application "Finder Liaison 1.0"
        copy (a reference to Disk "Thendara") to folderName
end tell
fileWalker(folderName)


on fileWalker(currentFolder)
        tell application "Finder Liaison 1.0"
                repeat with currentFile in (Get Files in currentFolder)
                        beep
                end repeat
        end tell
end fileWalker
```

This script uses the shortcut you learned in the last section: placing a command in parentheses within another, and using the first command's result in the enclosing command. In this case, it simply beeps once for every file on the top level of your hard drive.

Since the repeat loop uses the list information to place a value in "currentFile," you can use a conditional within the repeat loop to see if the text in currentFile ends with " alias."

```
tell application "Finder Liaison 1.0"
    copy (a reference to Disk "Thendara") to folderName
end tell
fileWalker(folderName)


on fileWalker(currentFolder)
    tell application "Finder Liaison 1.0"
        repeat with currentFile in (Get Files in currentFolder)
            if currentFile ends with " alias" then beep
        end repeat
    end tell
end fileWalker
```

Run this script. If you've only one file on the top level of your hard drive that ends with " alias," the computer should have beeped once.

However, you don't want the computer to simply beep when it finds a file that ends with " alias." You want to remove the text from the end of the filename.

## Changing the Name: An Introduction to Workarounds

AppleScript enables you to add two pieces of text together, but there's no easy way to remove one piece of text from another. This poses a problem, since your script should remove the text " alias" from a larger chunk of text (the name of the file). A workaround is necessary.

COMPLEX SCRIPTS: CLIMBING THE MOUNTAIN


Workarounds are like detours: a way to get where you're going when you can't get there directly. Frequently, a command or application won't do *exactly* what you want it to do. If you're willing to think of ways around the limitation, there is usually a solution.

In order to work around this limitation, you can use one of the scripting additions supplied with part of the AppleScript package. The "String Commands" scripting addition has a command called "offset" that enables you to determine how many characters into a string another string starts. You use it by writing something like:

---

offset of "Tao" in "The Tao of AppleScript"

---

This command puts the number 5 into the result window. The string "Tao" starts on the fifth character of the string "The Tao of AppleScript" (space characters count). If the first string is not contained by the other string, the command returns a zero.

With this command, rather than removing " alias" from the end of the filename, you rename the file with the characters up to " alias." If you have a file named "AppleScript alias," you rename the file using characters 1 through 11, avoiding the string " alias" that starts on the twelfth character.

Before setting the name of the file, take a look at the result of this "formula" using an alias titled "zebra alias." (In this script, you must use a file with a character that comes late in the alphabet, as the result window shows only the last item checked).

---

```
tell application "Finder Liaison 1.0"
     copy (a reference to Disk "Thendara") to folderName
end tell
fileWalker(folderName)

on fileWalker(currentFolder)
     tell application "Finder Liaison 1.0"
```

```
        repeat with currentFile in (Get Files in currentFolder)
            if currentFile ends with " alias" then
                characters 1 thru ((the offset of " alias" in
                currentFile) - 1) of currentFile
            end if
        end repeat
    end tell
end fileWalker
```

When you run this script, the result window contains a list where each item is a character in the variable "currentFile." This isn't exactly what you were looking for. To correct this, you must coerce the list to a string. This concatenates the items in the list into one long string. Coercing {"A", "p", "p", "l", "e"} to a string would result in "Apple." Here's what the new script looks like:

```
tell application "Finder Liaison 1.0"
    copy (a reference to Disk "Thendara") to folderName
end tell
fileWalker(folderName)

on fileWalker(currentFolder)
    tell application "Finder Liaison 1.0"

        repeat with currentFile in (Get Files in currentFolder)
            if currentFile ends with " alias" then
                (characters 1 thru ((the offset of " alias" in
                currentFile) - 1) of currentFile) as string
            end if
        end repeat
    end tell
end fileWalker
```

The entire phrase must be placed within parentheses so that AppleScript knows to convert the entire result to a string. Finally, you must use Finder Liaison's "Set Name of" command to change the name of the file:

```
tell application "Finder Liaison 1.0"
     copy (a reference to Disk "Thendara") to folderName
end tell
fileWalker(folderName)


on fileWalker(currentFolder)
     tell application "Finder Liaison 1.0"
          repeat with currentFile in (Get Files in currentFolder)
               if currentFile ends with " alias" then
                    Set Name of File currentFile in currentFolder to
                    (characters 1 thru ((the offset of " alias" in
                    currentFile) - 1) of currentFile) as string
               end if
          end repeat
     end tell
end fileWalker
```

When you run this script, the Finder Liaison returns an error. Why? This is because of an oddity in AppleScript. When you perform a repeat loop that traverses a list, AppleScript doesn't exactly set the counting variable to the value in the list, but rather sets it to something like "item 1 of {1,2,3,4}." AppleScript has no problem with this, since it understands what "items in a list" are. Unfortunately, it passes this "modified value" to applications when you use the counting variable.

So what Finder Liaison actually gets from AppleScript with this command is "Set Name of File (item 1 of {"AppleShare PDS","Desktop DB","Desktop DF","zebra alias"}) etc." Finder Liaison doesn't know what "items in a list" are, so it returns an error.

Again, you'll need to use a workaround. You need to coerce "currentFile" to a string when you refer to it. This forces AppleScript to make the counting variable into text. (After running this script, you will need to close and then open your hard drive's window to see the name change.)

```
tell application "Finder Liaison 1.0"
    copy (a reference to Disk "Thendara") to folderName
end tell
fileWalker(folderName)


on fileWalker(currentFolder)
    tell application "Finder Liaison 1.0"
        repeat with currentFile in (Get Files in currentFolder)
            if currentFile ends with " alias" then
                Set Name of File (currentFile as string) in
                currentFolder to (characters 1 thru ((the offset of
                "alias" in currentFile) - 1) of currentFile) as string
            end if
        end repeat
    end tell
end fileWalker
```

This script removed the " alias" from any files on the top level of the hard drive. Next, you'll adapt it to go through your hard drive and remove " alias" from all the files. For this, you need to tell the script to look into folders as well as at the top level of your hard drive.

## Peeking Inside Folders

Remember, a directory traversal moves its way through folders, executing the same commands on each folder. You need to come up with a vehicle that moves from one folder to another.

First you'll need to get a list of all the folders. Finder Liaison does this with the "Get Folders in" command, which works like the "Get Files in" command you just used:

## Get Folders in currentFolder

You'll need to set up a repeat loop that runs once for each item in a list of folders. The repeat loop's counting variable (subfolder) will be equal to the name of each folder in turn, so that the script beeps once for each folder in the current folder:

```
repeat with subFolder in (Get Folders in currentFolder)
    beep
end repeat
```

Once you have the folder's name, of course, you'll want to execute the commands in this subroutine on the files and folders within that folder, instead of just beeping.

This can be done by calling the subroutine from within the repeat loop (which is within the subroutine itself). Each time a subroutine gets called, even if it's already running, AppleScript behaves as if it is an entirely new set of commands. When it finishes that subroutine, it returns to the subroutine that called it and picks up where it left off.

You can see that doing this for every folder and every folder within those folders, etc., results in looking at every file on your entire hard drive. When the script reaches a point where there are only files in a folder, it moves on to the next folder in that folder's parent folder and keeps moving through the repeat loop for that folder. When it finishes with every item in the parent folder, it backs out again and looks inside the next folder in the list at that level, continuing until it finishes with all the files and folders on your hard drive.

Remember that the reference placed in the argument (a reference to Disk Thendara of Application Finder Liaison) of the subroutine (fileWalker) can point to a folder just as easily as to your hard drive. You can exploit this within the repeat loop by calling fileWalker with the argument being the path to the current folder within the hard drive. Your initial thought may be to type something like this.

```
fileWalker(a reference to Folder (subFolder as string) in
currentFolder)
```

However, remember that you can't put the command "fileWalker" within the "tell" statement, because AppleScript will attempt to send this command to the application. Earlier, you could move the command out of the tell statement. However, that won't work here because you enclose the entire subroutine in a "tell" statement. AppleScript provides a solution, however. You may remember learning about the special variable "me" in Chapter 2, "Scripting Basics." In AppleScript, "me" refers to the script itself. You can send a message to "me" using the "tell" command in the same way you can send a message to an application.

Send the "fileWalker" message to "me" so that AppleScript won't try to send the message to Finder Liaison:

```
tell me to fileWalker(a reference to Folder (subFolder as string)
in currentFolder)
```

## Make It Better

Since the purpose of scripting is to have your Mac do things without your supervision, you should concentrate on building safety features into a script.

This script will search through your entire hard drive. The capability to look at every file and folder and act upon it is a valuable scripting tool, but it also can be a dangerous tool. A script left unattended while working on files in the Finder can have disastrous results.

Always consider safety when working with directory traversals. Remember that you are working with the files on the hard drive and that you need to make sure nothing will go wrong. It is not very important with this script as you are only changing the names of files. But you may end up using this script as a model for other, more powerful directory traversals.

## Safety Considerations: Always Look Before You Leap

What happens if a person has an item that ends with " alias" but isn't an alias? One safeguard is already built in; the script won't affect a folder that ends with " alias," as it only affect files.

But what if a file ends with " Alias," with a capital A? Since the Finder does not assign a capital A when attaching the name alias to files, this is probably not simply another alias. AppleScript doesn't consider case when comparing strings, so a file with such an ending would be renamed. You can prevent this by placing a "considering" statement around the conditional to make AppleScript look at the case of the two strings as a criterion:

```
tell application "Finder Liaison 1.0"
    copy (a reference to Disk "Thendara") to folderName
end tell
fileWalker(folderName)


on fileWalker(currentFolder)
    tell application "Finder Liaison 1.0"
        repeat with currentFile in (Get Files in currentFolder)
            considering case
                if currentFile ends with " alias" then
                    Set Name of File (currentFile as string) in
                    currentFolder to (characters 1 thru ((the offset
                    of " alias" in currentFile) - 1) of currentFile) as
                    string
                end if
            end considering
        end repeat
```

```
          repeat with subFolder in (Get Folders in currentFolder)
              tell me to fileWalker(a reference to Folder (subFolder
                 as string) in currentFolder)
          end repeat
       end tell
    end fileWalker
```

Also, each alias contains one 'alis' resource, that has the same name as the file itself. If you set up a conditional that tests this criterion as well as the other two, you can be reasonably sure a file is an alias before the script changes its name. You'll be using the ResMover scripting addition, that you've already used, to verify whether the file you're working with is in fact an alias.

To find out if the file contains an 'alis' resource, use ResMover's "Get resource types" command to generate list of all the types of resources within a given file. You can then act on this file only if there is an 'alis' resource in the list returned. Combine this with your existing conditional by using an "and" modifier.

Remember that ResMover uses file references to point to files on your hard drive. Finder Liaison has the capability to convert its method of looking at files to the standard file references that ResMover uses. You can use the path of the file from aFinder Liaison to generate a file reference that can be passed to ResMover.

```
considering case
    if (currentFile ends with " alias") and ((get resource types in
    File (Get Path of File (currentFile as string) in currentFolder))
    contains {"alis"}) then
        Set Name of File (currentFile as string) in currentFolder to
        (characters 1 thru ((the offset of " alias" in currentFile) - 1)
        of currentFile) as string
    end if
end considering
```

You'll notice that when you compiled the script, the word "File" was capitalized. This is because the word "File" has special meaning to Finder Liaison (the current target of the tell statement). In order to make this into a file reference, you must use the word "alias" in place of "file", as in:

```
if (currentFile ends with " alias") and ((get resource types in alias
(Get Path of File (currentFile as string) in currentFolder)) con-
tains {"alis"}) then
```

Checking for 'alis' resources is only the first step. You also must check if the first 'alis' resource in the file has the same name as the file itself by getting the name of a resource with ResMover:

```
considering case
    if (currentFile ends with " alias") and ((get resource types in
    alias (Get Path of File (currentFile as string) in currentFolder))
    contains {"alis"}) and ((get name of resource number 1 of type
    "alis" in alias (Get Path of File (currentFile as string) in
    currentFolder) ) is currentFile) then
        Set Name of File (currentFile as string) in currentFolder to
        (characters 1 thru ((the offset of " alias" in currentFile) - 1)
        of currentFile) as string
    end if
end considering
```

Now, the conditional will be true only if the filename ends with " alias," the file contains an 'alis' resource, and the name of the first 'alis' resource is the same as the file itself.

The chances of this script renaming a non-alias file are quite remote. Nevertheless, you still may want to confirm the action of renaming when you run the script.

## When in Doubt, Ask

If you're writing a script that can do some real damage to a set of files, you should make sure that anyone using the script can oversee the actions and stop the script, if necessary. One way of doing this is to use a dialog to confirm each renaming.

AppleScript provides a mechanism for showing simple dialogs with the scripting addition "display dialog." This is part of the standard AppleScript package, so it's already in your "Scripting Additions" folder.

The command "display dialog" presents a dialog box with a prompt that you specify, providing "OK" and "Cancel" buttons. Place this single command into an empty script window:

```
display dialog "Do you really wish to rename this file?"
```

When you run this script, you'll see that you get a dialog box with the question you specified (see figure 8.1).

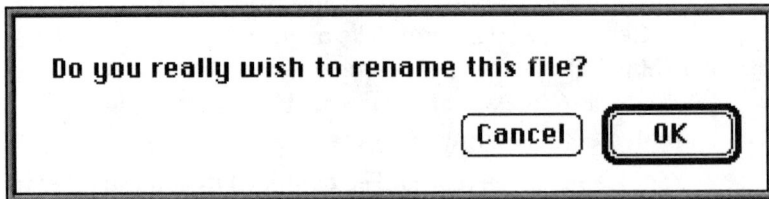

*Figure 8.1*
*Using the display dialog command.*

While this is nice, but you may want to provide a bit more information. You could ask the question and display the name of the file that is about to be acted upon. This information is already available in the variable "currentFile." Simply place the variable into the prompt of the dialog and place this line into the script we've been building up.

```
display dialog "Are you sure you wish to rename " & currentFile & "?"
```

You'll notice that when you run this script, pressing Cancel results in the file being renamed anyway. You must instruct the script to look at which button was pressed.

When you dismiss the dialog box, AppleScript returns a record that contains information about what happened in the dialog box.

One of the items it returns is labeled "button returned" and it contains the name of the button that was pressed. You can see this by returning the script that displays the dialog, and then displaying the result window.

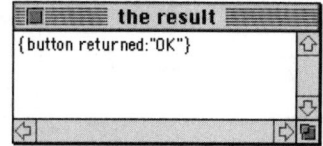

```
▭▭▭▭ the result ▭▭▭▭
{button returned:"OK"}
```

To see if the "OK" button was pressed, you'll need to put another conditional inside the first conditional that determines whether to change the file or not depending on whether or not the button pressed was "OK."

---

```
considering case
    if (currentFile ends with " alias") and ((get resource types in
    alias (Get Path of File (currentFile as string) in currentFolder))
    contains {"alis"}) and ((get name of resource number 1 of type
    "alis" in alias (Get Path of File (currentFile as string) in
    currentFolder)) is currentFile) then
        if the button returned of (display dialog "Are you sure you
        wish to rename " & currentFile & "?") is "OK" then
            Set Name of File (currentFile as string) in currentFolder
            to (characters 1 thru ((the offset of " alias" in
            currentFile) - 1) of currentFile) as string
        end if
    end if
end considering
```

---

Looking at the dialog box you displayed in this script, you may notice its buttons are a bit misleading. The "Cancel" button doesn't cancel the script, as its name implies. The "display dialog" command enables you to change the names of the buttons in the window. To do this, you must include a parameter named "buttons" and a list where each item is the name of a button in your dialog. To make your script clearer, you could name the button "Skip," as in:

```
if the button returned of (display dialog "Are you sure you wish to
rename " & currentFile & "?" buttons {"OK", "Skip"}) is "OK" then
```

```
     Set Name of File (currentFile as string) in currentFolder to
     (characters 1 thru ((the offset of " alias" in currentFile) - 1) of
     currentFile) as string
  end if
```

## Visual Feedback

The dialog you just set up will tell you only the name of the file you're about to rename. If you don't recognize the file by its name, you may not have any idea which file the dialog is referring to.

One way to fix this problem may be to actually show the file in the Finder as the script shows the dialog. You can do this by using Finder Liaison's "Reveal" command. This command opens a window and selects a particular icon.

To use this command, simply type "Reveal" and the path to the file, as in this conditional:

```
if (currentFile ends with " alias") and ((get resource types in alias
(Get Path of File (currentFile as string) in currentFolder)) contains
{"alis"}) and ((get name of resource number 1 of type "alis" in alias
(Get Path of File (currentFile as string) in currentFolder)) is
currentFile) then
     Reveal File (currentFile as string) in currentFolder
     if the button returned of (display dialog "Are you sure you
     wish to rename " & currentFile & "?" buttons {"OK", "Skip"})
     is "OK" then
          Set Name of File (currentFile as string) in currentFolder to
          (characters 1 thru ((the offset of " alias" in currentFile) - 1)
          of currentFile) as string
  end if
```

When the dialog box is displayed, the Finder will open the window the file is in and highlight the icon. (If necessary, the user can move the dialog box out of the way to look at the file.) This provides visual feedback to the user about which file will be changed.

If you do this for every file, you may end up with many open windows. Once you're finished with a window, you should close it using Finder Liaison's "Close Window of" command. You know which folder the current file is in, since it is the reference stored in currentFolder. Simply use the "Close Window of" command:

```
if (currentFile ends with " alias") and ((get resource types in alias
(Get Path of File (currentFile as string) in currentFolder)) contains
{"alis"}) and ((get name of resource number 1 of type "alis" in alias
(Get Path of File (currentFile as string) in currentFolder)) is
currentFile) then
    Reveal File (currentFile as string) in currentFolder
    if the button returned of (display dialog "Are you sure you
    wish to rename " & currentFile & "?" buttons {"OK", "Skip"})
    is "OK" then
        Set Name of File (currentFile as string) in currentFolder to
        (characters 1 thru ((the offset of " alias" in currentFile) - 1)
        of currentFile) as string
    end if
    Close Window of currentFolder
end if
```

## A Little Overkill Can't Hurt

You may find that all these safety features become cumbersome. You may want to leave out some safety features to make the script more automated or less specific. You should, however, consider what others may want your script to do.

## Fix the Bugs

Now that you've addressed some of the safety issues involved with directory traversal, you should look at some of its possible bugs.

You can now search through every file on your hard drive and perform a specific task on each. You also can be sure that every file and folder, even the invisible ones, will be found.

## Duplicate Filenames

This script still has at least one bug that could cause a problem. What happens if the script attempts to set a file to the same name as another file in the same folder? Well, you'll get an error.

You can prevent this by having the script check the names of the items in the folder. You already know how to get a list of all the files and folders within a folder. To find out if the name you're about to use is in either of those lists, you'll put the names of all the files and folders into one big list and see if the new string is contained in that list.

To create this list, you must concatenate the two lists obtained from Finder Liaison's "Get Files in" and "Get Folders in" commands. You should do this as soon as the script enters the subroutine for a given folder, as in the following script:

```
on fileWalker(currentFolder)
    tell application "Finder Liaison 1.0"
        copy (Get Files in currentFolder) & (Get Folders in currentFolder) to folderContents
```

This script, upon entering the subroutine, concatenates the result from the "Get Files" command and the result from the "Get Folders" command. This combined list is placed into a variable named "folderContents."

The next step is to see if the new string is already contained within the list in "folderContents." AppleScript provides the mechanism you will use to determine if one list is contained within another. Since you need to know if a filename is already used, you must enclose that name in braces and compare it to the list inside "folderContents."

The formula that determines what the filename will become after stripping " alias" has already been determined; you can use that same formula with a "not" modifier to pass over a file if any item in the folder has that name:

```
if (currentFile ends with " alias") and ((get resource types in alias
(Get Path of File (currentFile as string) in currentFolder)) contains
{"alis"}) and ((get name of resource number 1 of type "alis" in alias
(Get Path of File (currentFile as string) in currentFolder)) is
currentFile) then
    if not (folderContents contains {(characters 1 thru ((the offset
    of " alias" in currentFile) - 1) of currentFile) as string}) then
        Reveal File (currentFile as string) in currentFolder
        if the button returned of (display dialog "Are you sure you
        wish to rename " & currentFile & "?" buttons {"OK",
        "Skip"}) is "OK" then
            Set Name of File (currentFile as string) in currentFolder
            to (characters 1 thru ((the offset of " alias" in
            currentFile) - 1) of currentFile) as string
        end if
        Close Window of currentFolder
    end if
end if
```

As it is, this script will do nothing if the new name of the file is already in use. This may be a viable option for some scripts; however, in this case the script should perform some other function if the name is already being used.

You will need to use an "else" statement to accomplish this. The following conditional will beep if the new name of the file is already taken. To try it, select an icon on your main hard drive and make an alias of it, then run the script. Because the original file has the same name as the new name of the alias file, the script will beep rather than rename it:

```
if not (folderContents contains {(characters 1 thru ((the offset of
" alias" in currentFile) - 1) of currentFile) as string}) then
    Reveal File (currentFile as string) in currentFolder
    if the button returned of (display dialog "Are you sure you
    wish to rename " & currentFile & "?" buttons {"OK", "Skip"})
    is "OK" then
        Set Name of File (currentFile as string) in currentFolder to
        (characters 1 thru ((the offset of " alias" in currentFile) - 1)
        of currentFile) as string
    end if
    Close Window of currentFolder
else
    beep
end if
```

## When in Doubt, Ask

In order to make this script truly effective, you should bring up a dialog box that asks the user for an alternate name for the file. AppleScript's dialog command enables you to have a dialog box that contains a field in which the user can enter a value. This is the "default answer" parameter. It's set up so that you can display a dialog that already has a default value in the field. However, if you put the string "" into the default answer, it will show an empty field into which the user can type information.

This dialog box should be informative to the user, it should let the user know which file caused the dialog box to appear, what the problem is, and what the user is expected to do about it. For instance, you may want to present "I cannot rename the file "zebra alias" because the name "zebra" is already in use by an item in this folder. Please enter a new name."

As before, you should give the user the option of skipping the file altogether. Therefore, you must once again use the "buttons" parameter within the command.

## Cleaning Up

Before typing in these commands, take a look at the script. You may notice that the formula that generates the new name is used repeatedly. You may want to put the result of this formula into a variable. This is a particularly good idea if the information is the result of a lengthy formula such as this one. Putting the text into a variable can tidy up the script and reduce the amount of typing.

Put the result of this formula into a variable, "newName," and then use that variable any time you need that information. The new script looks like this:

```
tell application "Finder Liaison 1.0"
    copy (a reference to Disk "Thendara") to folderName
end tell
fileWalker(folderName)


on fileWalker(currentFolder)
    tell application "Finder Liaison 1.0"
        copy (Get Files in currentFolder) & (Get Folders in
        currentFolder) to folderContents
        repeat with currentFile in (Get Files in currentFolder)
            considering case
                if (currentFile ends with " alias") and ((get re-
                source types in alias (Get Path of File (currentFile as
                string) in currentFolder)) contains {"alis"}) and
                ((get name of resource number 1 of type "alis" in
                alias (Get Path of File (currentFile as string) in
                currentFolder)) is currentFile) then
                    copy (characters 1 thru ((the offset of " alias"
                    in currentFile) - 1) of currentFile) as string
                    to newName
                    if not (folderContents contains {newName}) then
                        Reveal File (currentFile as string) in
                        currentFolder
```

```
                                    if the button returned of (display dialog
                                    "Are you sure you wish to rename " &
                                    currentFile & "?" buttons {"OK", "Skip"})
                                    is "OK" then
                                        Set Name of File (currentFile as string)
                                        in currentFolder to newName
                                    end if
                                    Close Window of currentFolder
                            else
                                beep
                            end if
                        end if
                    end considering
                    repeat with subFolder in (Get Folders in currentFolder)
                        tell me to fileWalker(a reference to Folder
                        (subFolder as string) in currentFolder)
                    end repeat
                end repeat
            end tell
        end fileWalker
```

## Back to the Script

You can put the command that displays the dialog box inside the else statement, as follows:

```
if not (folderContents contains {newName}) then
    Reveal File (currentFile as string) in currentFolder
    if the button returned of (display dialog "Are you sure you
    wish to rename " & currentFile & "?" buttons {"OK", "Skip"})
    is "OK" then
        Set Name of File (currentFile as string) in currentFolder to
        newName
    end if
    Close Window of currentFolder
```

**else**

```
    display dialog "I cannot rename the file " & currentFile & "
    because the name " & newName & " is already taken. Please
    enter a new name." buttons {"OK", "Skip"} default answer ""
```

**end if**

The script will now display a dialog box that asks the user to enter a name for a file if the attempted name is already in use.

As yet, the script doesn't do anything with the information it gets from the dialog box. You must tell the script to do that. As before, the dialog box will return a record. This time, there will be an additional item in the record labeled "text returned." This item contains the information entered by the user. You should put the result of this dialog into a variable, "dialogResults:"

**else**

```
    copy (display dialog "I cannot rename the file " & currentFile &
    " because the name " & newName & " is already taken. Please
    enter a new name." buttons {"OK", "Skip"} default answer "")
    to dialogResults
```

**end if**

The next step is to use this information to rename the file. Again, you'll use the "Set Name of" command from Finder Liaison:

**else**

```
    copy (display dialog "I cannot rename the file " & currentFile &
    " because the name " & newName & " is already taken. Please
    enter a new name." buttons {"OK", "Skip"} default answer "")
    to dialogResults
    Set Name of File (currentFile as string) in currentFolder to (text
    returned of dialogResults)
```

**end if**

## Error Checking

An important part of writing any script is a process called "error checking." This process involves trying to anticipate every possible user action, and reacting appropriately to those actions.

An important aspect of error checking is accounting for any button a user may use to dismiss the dialog. When you anticipated that a user may press the "Skip" button, you implemented a simple form of error checking.

You must to do this for the dialog you just set up. You can do this by using a conditional, as you did before:

```
else
    copy (display dialog "I cannot rename the file " & currentFile &
    " because the name " & newName & " is already taken. Please
    enter a new name." buttons {"OK", "Skip"} default answer "")
    to dialogResults
        if the button returned of dialogResults is "OK" then
            Set Name of File (currentFile as string) in currentFolder to
            (text returned of dialogResults)
        end if
end if
```

A more difficult aspect of error checking is anticipating user error. For example, what happens if the user enters another name that already exists into the dialog box? Finder Liaison, once again, generates an error.

Anticipating that a user may type in an existing name enables you to prevent the script from returning another error. You can give the user a second chance, by setting up a conditional to check this newly entered value and displaying the dialog box once again if that new value is also already in use. Use the variable "folderContents" and the same dialog again:

```
else
    copy (display dialog "I cannot rename the file " & currentFile &
    " because the name " & newName & " is already taken. Please
    enter a new name." buttons {"OK", "Skip"} default answer "")
    to dialogResults
    if the button returned of dialogResults is "OK" then
        if folderContents contains {the text returned of
        dialogResults} then
            beep
            copy (display dialog "I can not rename the file " &
            currentFile & " because the name " & newName & " is
            already taken. Please enter a new name." buttons
            {"OK", "Skip"} default answer "") to dialogResults
        end if
        Set Name of File (currentFile as string) in currentFolder to
        (text returned of dialogResults)
    end if
end if
```

If the user presses "OK" and the name entered is already in use, the script will bring up the dialog box again.

But the user could still generate a Finder Liaison error by entering a name that already exists. To completely prevent this error, you must set up a repeat loop that will run whenever the text entered into the dialog box is a name that is already in use in that folder.

You must use AppleScript's "repeat until" command for this:

```
if folderContents contains {the text returned of dialogResults}
then
    repeat until not (folderContents contains {the text returned
    of dialogResults})
        beep
```

```
    copy (display dialog "I cannot rename the file " &
    currentFile & " because the name " & newName & " is
    already taken. Please enter a new name." buttons {"OK",
    "Skip"} default answer "") to dialogResults
  end repeat
end if
```

Now that you've handled this bug, you've added the flexibilty for the script to implement a series of steps to solve a problem, using input from the user to guide it.

## Make It Better

While this script is now complete, it serves only a very specific function: removing the word " alias" from alias files. That's useful, but you could use this script as a base to build a more powerful and more useful script—one that can find and replace text in the names of files and folders within the Finder based on two values: what to search for, and what to replace the result with.

The first step is to declare the two values. Put " alias" into the variable "findText" and "" into the variable "replaceText.":

```
copy " alias" to findText
copy "" to replaceText
tell application "Finder Liaison 1.0"
    copy (a reference to Disk "Thendara") to folderName
end tell
fileWalker(folderName)
```

Unfortunately, variables used in the main script are not available from within subroutines. The values of findText and replaceText will not be passed to the subroutine.

You could make them into arguments of the subroutine, as in:

```
fileWalker(folderName, findText, replaceText)
```

However, AppleScript provides "global variables" for variables that must be accessible from any part of a script.

Making global variables is simple. Every variable has the potential to become a global variable. Use the word "global" and follow it with a list of all the variables you wish to become global. In this case, you want to use both "findText" and "replaceText" as global variables. Global variables take more memory than standard variables, so you should use them sparingly.

It's conventional to declare all global variables at the beginning of the subroutine, so that you don't need to search through the script to find which ones are global. Here's how the initial lines of the subroutine look using the two global variables:

```
on fileWalker(currentFolder)
    global findText, replaceText
```

The subroutine now has access to those variables. If you change the values inside those variables, any part of the script that uses that variable will use the new value, although you need not do that for this script. This differs from variables local to a subroutine, that retain their values only in the subroutine. This is necessary for the directory traversal to function properly; when you deal with all the folders in a given folder, the original subroutine that called that subroutine still has its same value in "currentFolder." This is what enables the directory traversal to work its way back up.

Now that those variables are accessible, you must determine how to use that information in your script.

While this example script was designed to change specific text, a general-purpose script should be more flexible than to limit itself to simply the specific text. The first conditional should check if "currentFile" *contains* the text in "findText." You also should remove the comparisons that check whether a file is an alias— since you'll want to look at files and folders, regardless of whether they're aliases or not.

```
if currentFile contains findText then
    copy (characters 1 thru ((the offset of " alias" in currentFile) -
    1) of currentFile) as string to newName
    if not (folderContents contains {newName}) then
        Reveal File (currentFile as string) in currentFolder
        if the button returned of (display dialog "Are you sure you
        wish to rename " & currentFile & "?" buttons {"OK",
        "Skip"}) is "OK" then
            Set Name of File (currentFile as string) in currentFolder
            to newName
        end if
        Close Window of currentFolder
    else
        copy (display dialog "I cannot rename the file " &
        currentFile & " because the name " & newName & " is
        already taken. Please enter a new name." buttons {"OK",
        "Skip"} default answer "") to dialogResults
        if the button returned of dialogResults is "OK" then
            if folderContents contains {the text returned of
            dialogResults} then
                repeat until not (folderContents contains {the
                text returned of dialogResults})
                    beep
                    copy (display dialog "I cannot rename the file
                    " & currentFile & " because the name " &
                    newName & " is already taken. Please enter a
                    new name." buttons {"OK", "Skip"} default
                    answer "") to dialogResults
                end repeat
            end if
            Set Name of File (currentFile as string) in currentFolder
            to (text returned of dialogResults)
        end if
    end if
end if
```

You also need to change the information placed into "newName". The workaround you used was only good for removing the characters at the end of the string. Remember that the value you are searching for in this script with "findText" can be anywhere within the word. You need to take into account the fact that the text could be in the middle of the string.

To make a value for "newName," you need to use another workaround. To do a find and replace, you can think of it as dividing the original text into three parts. There are the characters that come before the text you're finding, the characters of text that you wish to replace, and the characters that come after the text you wish to replace.

To make a new name, concatenate the first part of the string with the text you want to use as a replacement. Then concatenate that to the third part of the result. You've essentially replaced the text you found with the new text.

The first two pieces of this puzzle are already available: you've written the part of the script that gives you all the characters preceding the found text and value of the replacement text is held in "replaceText."

The third piece is a little bit trickier. You still will want a range of characters, but no longer starting with the first character. You want the range of characters which starts with the character just after the text you want to replace and ends with the last character of the original filename.

The same scripting addition that provides you with the capability to get the offset of one string in another enables you to determine the length of a string in characters. This will be very useful for the third block of text you need to get.

The first thing you want to know about the third block is the position of its first character, which is also the character immediately after the block of text you want to replace. Consider for a moment how you would find the position of this character. If that block of text was at the beginning of the string, you would get the length of that block of text and add 1. For instance, for a file named " alias file," the character following " alias" is the length of " alias" plus 1.

In a file named "Another alias file," however, the block of text could fall anywhere within the name of the file. You must account for the offset of the text you want to replace. The character following " alias" is at position 14. The offset (the position of the first letter) of the string produces the number 8. If you then add the length of that string (6), and then 1, you'll be one character further than you should be. You must subtract one from the offset, then add the length, and then add 1. Obviously, subtracting one and adding one are mutually cancelling, so to get the position of the first character of the third block, you would simply add the offset of the block you're replacing, to the length of that block.

You can see how this works by typing the following script into a new script window:

```
characters ((the offset of "Tao" in "The Tao of AppleScript") +
(length of "Tao")) thru (length of "The Tao of AppleScript") of
"The Tao of AppleScript"
```

All the parentheses had to be used because AppleScript gets confused when it sees strings next to mathematical symbols. You have to enclose the commands which get the offset and the length in parentheses so AppleScript will evaluate those first and use the resulting number.

Combining this information with the text blocks (which you already know how to get), you get the following formula for placing information into "newName":

```
copy (characters 1 thru ((the offset of findText in currentFile) -
1) of currentFile) & replaceText & characters ((the offset of
findText in currentFile) + (length of findText)) thru (length of
currentFile) of currentFile as string to newName
```

This works fine for files, but folders may also contain the text you're looking for. You'll need to perform all these same commands, replacing "currentFile" with "subFolder," within the repeat loop that traverses the list of folders. Copy the appropriate lines and place them under the "folder" repeat loop. You'll need to change some of the dialogs and such since you're now working with a folder rather than a file.

```
repeat with subFolder in (Get Folders in currentFolder)
    considering case
        if subFolder contains findText then
            copy (characters 1 thru ((the offset of findText in
            subFolder) - 1) of subFolder) & replaceText &
            characters ((the offset of findText in subFolder) +
            (length of findText)) thru (length of subFolder) of
            subFolder as string to newName
            if not (folderContents contains {newName}) then
                Reveal Folder (subFolder as string) in currentFolder
                if the button returned of (display dialog "Are you
                sure you wish to rename " & subFolder & "?"
                buttons {"OK", "Skip"}) is "OK" then
                    Set Name of Folder (subFolder as string) in
                    currentFolder to newName
                end if
                Close Window of currentFolder
            else
                copy (display dialog "I cannot rename the file " &
                subFolder & " because the name " & newName &
                " is already taken. Please enter a new name."
                buttons {"OK", "Skip"} default answer "") to
dialogResults
                if the button returned of dialogResults is "OK"
                then
                    if folderContents contains {the text returned
                    of dialogResults} then
                        repeat until not (folderContents contains
                        {the text returned of dialogResults})
                            beep
```

```
                              copy (display dialog "I cannot rename
                              the file " & subFolder & " because the
                              name " & newName & " is already
                              taken. Please enter a new name."
                              buttons {"OK", "Skip"} default answer
                              "") to dialogResults
                       end repeat
                    end if
                    Set Name of Folder (subFolder as string) in
                    currentFolder to (text returned of
                    dialogResults)
               end if
            end if
         end if
      end considering
      tell me to fileWalker(a reference to Folder (subFolder as
      string) in currentFolder)
   end repeat
```

If you change the name of a folder, however, you will not be able to set up a reference to the folder name represented by "subFolder" as the folder named in the variable will seem to no longer exist. You must change the value in subFolder every time you set the name of a folder so that the value in subFolder reflects the new name.

```
if not (folderContents contains {newName}) then
   Reveal Folder (subFolder as string) in currentFolder
   if the button returned of (display dialog "Are you sure you
   wish to rename " & subFolder & "?" buttons {"OK", "Skip"}) is
   "OK" then
      Set Name of Folder (subFolder as string) in currentFolder
      to newName
      copy newName to subFolder
   end if
   Close Window of currentFolder
```

```
    else
        copy (display dialog "I cannot rename the file " & subFolder &
        " because the name " & newName & " is already taken. Please
        enter a new name." buttons {"OK", "Skip"} default answer "")
        to dialogResults
        if the button returned of dialogResults is "OK" then
            if folderContents contains {the text returned of
            dialogResults} then
                repeat until not (folderContents contains {the text
                returned of dialogResults})
                    beep
                    copy (display dialog "I cannot rename the file " &
                    subFolder & " because the name " & newName &
                    " is already taken. Please enter a new name."
                    buttons {"OK", "Skip"} default answer "") to
                    dialogResults
                end repeat
            end if
            Set Name of Folder (subFolder as string) in currentFolder
            to (text returned of dialogResults)
            copy newName to subFolder
        end if
    end if
```

Your script has become quite complicated. You can see how taking into account all these real-life variables can lead to a complex script. Nevertheless, considering every possible factor when designing a script will make your scripts extremely robust. It will also make your scripts more enjoyable to use, as they will be less prone to crashing even when users do unexpected things.

## Adding Another Dialog

Before you finish this script, there's one more thing to add. At the moment, you must go into the actual script to change the values in the findText and replaceText variables.

Ideally, this script would show a dialog box that the user can enter the text to be found and the text to replace it with. This would enable you to save the script as an application so that the script itself need never be seen.

You've seen how to use the "display dialog" scripting addition to show simple dialogs, but they aren't powerful enough for this final touch. You need a dialog with two fields and a caption describing each field.

There is a scripting addition named "DialogRunner" provided on the disk with this book that enables you to display dialog resources stored in files. Also provided is a file named "Find and Replace Dialog" that contains a dialog for this script. It's in the same folder as the "Tao Sounds" file used previously.

To use DialogRunner, install it into the Scripting Additions folder and restart your Macintosh. This will enable AppleScript to see the addition.

The command to use, "run dialog," must contain the name of the dialog resource, a reference to the file in which that resource is stored, and a list that tells the addition which items will dismiss the dialog.

The dialog you'll be using is named "Find and Replace" and is stored in the "Find and Replace Dialog" file. You'll want the dialog to be dismissed when the user presses either the "OK" or "Cancel" button. The resulting command would look something like this (any variation would be in the name of your hard drive and the path to the particular file):

```
run dialog "Find and Replace" from file
"Thendara:Scripting:Scripting Tools:Find and Replace Dialog"
until {"OK", "Cancel"}
```

When you run a dialog, DialogRunner returns a record with several items. The first is labeled "item hit," and contains the name of the button pressed. The second is labeled "edit texts" and is a list of all values entered into the field in the order in which they're numbered in the dialog. In the case of the find and replace dialog, the first field in the list is the text to find and the second field in the list is the text to replace it with. DialogRunner also returns a list of the values of all checkboxes in the dialog and a list that describes which radio button was pressed in each group of radio buttons. You won't be using that information in this instance, since the dialog doesn't have checkboxes or radio buttons.

To add this dialog to the script, you need to do several things. First, call the dialog as you saw above. Second, run all the other commands only if the button pressed was "OK," as you've been doing with the dialogs AppleScript provides. The final step is to place the information from the fields into the appropriate variables.

Copy the information from the dialog into the variable "dialogResults." That variable can be used at other points in the script, but it's only used within subroutines, and you since you won't be calling it as a global variable, it won't be a problem. As far as AppleScript is concerned, they're not the same variables.

After making all those changes to the script, you end up with:

```
copy (run dialog "Find and Replace" from file
"Thendara:Scripting:Scripting Tools:Find and Replace Dialog" until
{"OK", "Cancel"}) to dialogResults
if the item hit of dialogResults is "OK" then
    copy (item 1 of the edit texts of dialogResults) to findText
    copy (item 2 of the edit texts of dialogResults) to replaceText
end if
tell application "Finder Liaison 1.0"
    copy (a reference to Disk "Thendara") to folderName
end tell
fileWalker(folderName)


on fileWalker(currentFolder)
    global findText, replaceText
```

```
tell application "Finder Liaison 1.0"
    copy (Get Files in currentFolder) & (Get Folders in
    currentFolder) to folderContents
    repeat with currentFile in (Get Files in currentFolder)
        considering case
            if currentFile contains findText then
                copy (characters 1 thru ((the offset of findText
                in currentFile) - 1) of currentFile) & replaceText
                & characters ((the offset of findText in
                currentFile) + (length of findText)) thru
                (length of currentFile) of currentFile as string
                to newName
                if not (folderContents contains {newName})
                then
                    Reveal File (currentFile as string) in
                    currentFolder
                    if the button returned of (display dialog
                    "Are you sure you wish to rename " &
                    currentFile & "?" buttons {"OK", "Skip"})
                    is "OK" then
                        Set Name of File (currentFile as string)
                        in currentFolder to newName
                    end if
                    Close Window of currentFolder
                else
                    copy (display dialog "I cannot rename the
                    file " & currentFile & " because the name "
                    & newName & " is already taken. Please
                    enter a new name." buttons {"OK",
                    "Skip"} default answer "") to dialogResults
                    if the button returned of dialogResults is
                    "OK" then
                        if folderContents contains {the text
                        returned of dialogResults} then
                            repeat until not (folderContents
                            contains {the text returned of
                            dialogResults})
                                beep
```

```
                    copy (display
                    dialog "I cannot
                    rename the file "
                    & currentFile & "
                    because the name
                    " & newName & "
                    is already taken.
                    Please enter a new
                    name." buttons
                    {"OK", "Skip"}
                    default answer "")
                    to dialogResults
               end repeat
          end if
          Set Name of File (currentFile as string)
          in currentFolder to (text returned of
          dialogResults)
        end if
      end if
    end if
  end considering
end repeat
repeat with subFolder in (Get Folders in currentFolder)
  considering case
    if subFolder contains findText then
        copy (characters 1 thru ((the offset of findText
        in subFolder) - 1) of subFolder) & replaceText
        & characters ((the offset of findText in
        subFolder) + (length of findText)) thru (length
        of subFolder) of subFolder as string to
        newName
        if not (folderContents contains {newName})
        then
            Reveal Folder (subFolder as string) in
            currentFolder
            if the button returned of (display dialog
            "Are you sure you wish to rename " &
            subFolder & "?" buttons {"OK", "Skip"}) is
            "OK" then
```

```
            Set Name of Folder (subFolder as
            string) in currentFolder to newName
            copy newName to subFolder
        end if
        Close Window of currentFolder
    else
        copy (display dialog "I cannot rename the
        file " & subFolder & " because the name "
        & newName & " is already taken. Please
        enter a new name." buttons {"OK",
        "Skip"} default answer "") to dialogResults
        if the button returned of dialogResults is
        "OK" then
            if folderContents contains {the text
            returned of dialogResults} then
                repeat until not (folderContents
                contains {the text returned of
                dialogResults})
                    beep
                    copy (display
                    dialog "I cannot
                    rename the file "
                    & subFolder & "
                    because the name
                    " & newName & "
                    is already taken.
                    Please enter a new
                    name." buttons
                    {"OK", "Skip"}
                    default answer "")
                to dialogResults
                end repeat
            end if
            Set Name of Folder (subFolder as
            string) in currentFolder to (text
            returned of dialogResults)
            copy newName to subFolder
```

```
                    end if
                  end if
                end if
              end considering
              tell me to fileWalker(a reference to Folder (subFolder
                as string) in currentFolder)
            end repeat
          end tell
        end fileWalker
```

This script first displays the dialog for entering information. If you press OK, the script copies the necessary information into the two variables and calls the subroutine. That's it.

## On Your Own

Congratulations! You've successfully completed the largest script in this book. Go ahead and save it as a script application, and you'll never need to look at this script again. (Unless, of course, you think of more features to add!)

Having made it through the final leg of your journey, take time to play. Try different kinds of directory traversals. You could make a version of Sound Sucker that enables folders to be dragged onto it, so that it goes through every file in that folder to extract sounds. Be creative! Explore!

The next chapter is a description of advanced AppleScript features. You'll learn to use programs available over a network in your scripts, to fully exploit the power of subroutines, and to design your own objects which contain script commands.

# *Reaching the Summit*

The scripting skills you have learned have enabled you to auto-mate large tasks, design new utilities—virtually anything you want to do! But AppleScript has even more capabilities that can increase your scripting power dramatically.

These capabilities, which are similar to "true" programming language functions, include: the capability to write commands that sound like everyday English phrases; script objects, which are like subroutines except that you can access them from many different scripts; and the capability to reach out across a network to use applications running on other Macs.

## "Nearly English" Subroutines

In the previous section, you saw subroutines used for fairly com-plex actions or functions. You may have noticed that the commands used to call subroutines don't resemble English sentences:

```
on average(listofNums)
```

The AppleScript commands you've learned sound almost like normal English, such as:

---

set the contents of window 1 of application "Scriptable Text Editor" to "The Tao of AppleScript"

---

Fortunately, AppleScript enables you to create subroutines that you call in a more English-like syntax. Look again at the subroutine that averages a list of numbers, from the previous section:

---

**copy** (average({2, 3, 4, 5})) **to** avgResult
display dialog avgResult


**on** average(listofNums)
    **copy** 0 **to** total
    **repeat with** currentNumber in listofNums
        **copy** currentNumber + total to total
    **end repeat**
    **return** total ÷ (**the** number **of** items **in** listofNums)
**end** average

---

Unless you know what to look for, it's not immediately apparent that "on average(listofNums)" is even a command. Using "on" makes it look like a conditional. One way to make it more understandable is to use the word "to" instead of "on" in the line that introduces the subroutine:

---

**copy** (average({2, 3, 4, 5})) **to** avgResult
display dialog avgResult

**to** average(listOfNums)
    **copy** 0 **to** total
    **repeat with** currentNumber in listOfNums
        **copy** currentNumber + total **to** total

```
    end repeat
    return total ÷ (the number of items in listOfNums)
end average
```

This script makes a bit more sense. You are closer to stating, "to average this list of numbers, do this," but it's a fairly minor change. The parentheses still make this command stand out as odd among the other commands in the subroutine.

```
copy (average({2, 3, 4, 5})) to avgResult
```

You don't need these parentheses around listofNums. Instead, you can use a wide range of labels to make the command feel more English-like. You can, for instance, use the word "of" in the first line of this subroutine:

```
copy (average({2, 3, 4, 5})) to avgResult
display dialog avgResult
```

```
to average of listOfNums
    copy 0 to total
    repeat with currentNumber in listOfNums
        copy currentNumber + total to total
    end repeat
    return total ÷ (the number of items in listOfNums)
end average
```

When you call the subroutine, it will look more natural, as in the following script:

```
copy (average of {2, 3, 4, 5}) to avgResult
display dialog avgResult
```

You can see that this looks more like the AppleScript commands you're used to seeing. You're telling the script to "put the average of {2,3,4,5} into the variable named avgResult," as it implies. Further, you can name your subroutine more descriptively, such as "getAverage." This almost makes the first line of the script into a real English sentence:

```
to getAverage of listOfNums
```

AppleScript gives you a wide variety of words to use as labels that help you make English-like sentences to call your subroutines. The following words are recognized as labels: at, from, to, for, thru, through, by, on, into, onto, between, against, out of, instead of, aside from, around, beside, beneath, under, over, above, below, apart from.

For instance, you could write a subroutine to make Progress Bar count from one number to another:

```
to moveProgressBar(low, high, interval)
    tell application "Progress Bar 1.0"
        make new window
        tell window 1
            set the minimum value of progress bar 1 to low
            set the maximum value of progress bar 1 to high
            repeat with i from low to high by interval
                set the current value of progress bar 1 to i
            end repeat
        end tell
        quit
    end tell
end moveProgressBar
```

However, this script is awkward and counterintuitive. It is also difficult to remember which argument goes where. Using labels, you can make this subroutine more natural-sounding:

```
to moveProgressBar from low to high by interval
    tell application "Progress Bar 1.0"
        make new window
        tell window 1
            set the minimum value of progress bar 1 to low
            set the maximum value of progress bar 1 to high
            repeat with i from low to high by interval
                set the current value of progress bar 1 to i
            end repeat
        end tell
        quit
    end tell
end moveProgressBar
```

Not only is a call to this subroutine more intuitive, but you'll also have no problem remembering the order of the arguments, since it is a natural English phrase:

```
moveProgressBar from 1 to 100 by 10
```

You're stuck with making the name of the subroutine one word. You can, however, apply the same rules as those for variable names and use underscore characters to represent spaces, as in:

```
move_Progress_Bar from 1 to 100 by 10
to move_Progress_Bar from low to high by interval
    tell application "Progress Bar 1.0"
        make new window
        tell window 1
            set the minimum value of progress bar 1 to low
            set the maximum value of progress bar 1 to high
            repeat with i from low to high by interval
                set the current value of progress bar 1 to i
```

```
            end repeat
         end tell
         quit
      end tell
   end move_Progress_Bar
```

AppleScript provides yet another powerful method for making subroutines easier to read and call. You can use the term "given," followed by labels, to establish arguments. When you define the subroutine, you attach a variable to the label. Then, when you call the subroutine, the value with the same label will be placed in the variable. For instance, you may rewrite your progress bar subroutine in the following way:

```
to move_Progress_Bar given lowNumber:low, highNumber:high,
intervalNumber:interval
   tell application "Progress Bar 1.0"
      make new window
      tell window 1
         set the minimum value of progress bar 1 to low
         set the maximum value of progress bar 1 to high
         repeat with i from low to high by interval
            set the current value of progress bar 1 to i
         end repeat
      end tell
      quit
   end tell
end move_Progress_Bar
```

To call this subroutine from the main script, you would write:

```
move_Progress_Bar given lowNumber:1, highNumber:100,
intervalNumber:10
```

When the script runs, it takes the value attached to the label "lowNumber" and places that in the variable named "low" in the subroutine.

You may think this is not very intuitive, especially when compared to other methods. However, this capability is useful when one or more of the labels has a Boolean value attached to it. You then no longer must say "given," but rather you can use the words "with" and "without." If you use "with" when calling the subroutine, AppleScript sets the value of those labels to true. If you use "without," it sets the labels you list to false.

For instance, you might have an option to have your subroutine beep when it's finished:

```
to move_Progress_Bar from low to high by interval given
beeping:beepingValue
    tell application "Progress Bar 1.0"
        make new window
        tell window 1
            set the minimum value of progress bar 1 to low
            set the maximum value of progress bar 1 to high
            repeat with i from low to high by interval
                set the current value of progress bar 1 to i
            end repeat
        end tell
        quit
    end tell
    if beepingValue is true then beep
end move_Progress_Bar
```

If you want to call this subroutine and have it beep when finished, you would write:

```
move_Progress_Bar from 1 to 100 by 10 given beeping:true
```

When you compile this script, you'll see that AppleScript rewrites your script command:

---

move_Progress_Bar from 1 to 100 by 10 **with** beeping

---

By using the word "with," you tell AppleScript to call this subroutine and set the value attached to the "beeping" label (the variable "beepingValue") to true.

If you don't want the subroutine to beep when it finishes, you would use "without:"

---

move_Progress_Bar from 1 to 100 by 10 **without** beeping

---

When you call the subroutine, the value of the variable attached to the label "beeping" is set to false.

You can combine a long string of labels by using "with" and "without" and "and." If you have four labels—for example, "beeping," "ticking," "quitting," and "stopping"—and want the first two set to true and the second two set to false, you can call that subroutine with the following command:

---

subroutineName **with** beeping **and** ticking **without** quitting **and** stopping

---

To declare a subroutine with multiple labels, simply separate the labels by commas.

AppleScript affords you a great deal of flexibility when you define subroutines. You can set them up so that they read just like normal AppleScript commands and natural English phrases. This way, you can make your subroutine commands as easy to use as AppleScript itself.

## Script Objects

You may have subroutines that you use repeatedly in your scripts. You may want to group these commonly used subroutines so you can access access them from several scripts.

AppleScript gives you this capability with script objects. You can tell script applications to execute certain actions, and even set properties within them. They enable you to group multiple subroutines into a single object that can be addressed from within a script, without having to copy the subroutines into many script files.

You've seen how a simple subroutine can average a list of numbers. What if there are several subroutines that do other statistical manipulations? You may have a script such as the following, that finds the maximum number in a list of numbers:

```
to findMax of listofNums
    copy 0 to greatest
    repeat with i in listofNums
        if i > greatest then copy i to greatest
    end repeat
    return greatest
end findMax
```

You might use this subroutine frequently in your scripts, and would probably find it awkward to copy it from one script to another over and over. Instead, you can set up a script object that contains both of these subroutines, so that you can access them from any script.

To define a script object, you go through a process similar to defining a subroutine. First, you must name the object, say "statistics."

To make sure AppleScript understands that this is a script object, you must use the word "script" in the same way you used the word "on" and "to." For instance, to make a script object named "statistics," you would write the following in a separate script file:

```
script statistics
end script
```

With script object definitions, you don't end with the name, as you did with subroutines, but with the word "script."

To put both subroutines into this script object, copy the text and insert it within the script object after the "script statistics" statement, but before the "end script" command.

```
script statistics
    to average of listofNums
        copy 0 to total
        repeat with currentNumber in listofNums
            copy currentNumber + total to total
        end repeat
        return total ÷ (the number of items in listofNums)
    end average
    to findMax of listofNums
        copy 0 to greatest
        repeat with i in listofNums
            if i > greatest then copy i to greatest
        end repeat
    end findMax
end script
```

Both these subroutines are now part of the script object.

To access these subroutines, you must use the "tell" command with the name of the script object. Type this into the same script window as the statistics script object:

```
tell statistics
    average of {2, 3, 4, 5}
end tell
```

```
script statistics
    to average of listofNums
```

```
        copy 0 to total
        repeat with currentNumber in listofNums
            copy currentNumber + total to total
        end repeat
        return total ÷ (the number of items in listofNums)
    end average
    to findMax of listofNums
        copy 0 to greatest
        repeat with i in listofNums
            if i > greatest then copy i to greatest
        end repeat
    end findMax
end script
```

Running this script will result in the script using the statistics script object to get the average of the list of numbers you sent it.

You'll see that both of these subroutines use the same type of argument: a list of numbers. Though it's easy to include this when calling the subroutine, you may want to set up a list of numbers and then run a set of commands on it.

AppleScript enables you to assign "properties" to the script objects. These act as global variables for all the subroutines in that script object. They are much like properties of objects, such as the font property of a word.

To set a property, type the word "property" followed by that particular property's name (again, using all the same rules that apply to variable names), a colon, and an initial value of the property. For instance, to make a property for a list of numbers, you would do the following:

```
script statistics
    property listofNums : {}
    to average of listofNums
```

```
        copy 0 to total
        repeat with currentNumber in listofNums
            copy currentNumber + total to total
        end repeat
        return total ÷ (the number of items in listofNums)
    end average
    to findMax of listofNums
        copy 0 to greatest
        repeat with i in listofNums
            if i > greatest then copy i to greatest
        end repeat
    end findMax
end script
```

Because the list of numbers is now in a global variable, you can
remove it from the definitions of the subroutines. You do, however, need to tell AppleScript that you'll be using that variable
globally:

```
script statistics
    property listofNums : {}
    to average( )
        global listofNums
        copy 0 to total
        repeat with currentNumber in listofNums
            copy currentNumber + total to total
        end repeat
        return total ÷ (the number of items in listofNums)
    end average
    to findMax( )
        global listofNums
        copy 0 to greatest
```

```
            repeat with i in listofNums
                if i > greatest then copy i to greatest
            end repeat
        end findMax
    end script
```

You'll notice that, because you no longer have special labels for the arguments, AppleScript will put empty parentheses after the names of the subroutines.

To change the value of a property, you can use the set command, as you've learned to do with other objects:

```
tell statistics
    set listofNums to {2, 3, 4, 5}
    average( )
end tell


script statistics
    property listofNums : {}
    to average( )
        global listofNums
        copy 0 to total
        repeat with currentNumber in listofNums
            copy currentNumber + total to total
        end repeat
        return total ÷ (the number of items in listofNums)
    end average
    to findMax( )
        global listofNums
        copy 0 to greatest
        repeat with i in listofNums
            if i > greatest then copy i to greatest
```

```
        end repeat
    end findMax
end script
```

Now that you know how to construct script objects, you'll want to access them from any script. To do this, you must save the script file without the "script" and "end script" commands. To make a "statistics" file, for instance, you would save the following script:

```
property listofNums : {}
to average( )
    global listofNums
    copy 0 to total
    repeat with currentNumber in listofNums
        copy currentNumber + total to total
    end repeat
    return total ÷ (the number of items in listofNums)
end average
to findMax( )
    global listofNums
    copy 0 to greatest
    repeat with i in listofNums
        if i > greatest then copy i to greatest
    end repeat
end findMax
```

When you want to use a script object, you must use the "load script" command to load the information from a file. To do so, you must give AppleScript a reference to a file. If you had a script file named "statistics" in a folder named "Scripting libraries" in your "Scripting" folder, you would use the following command:

```
load script file "Thendara:Scripting:Scripting libraries:statistics"
```

After loading the script, however, you must put the result into a variable that represents the name of the script object. For instance, you could refer to the script object as "statistics," in which case you'd write the following:

```
copy (load script file "Thendara:Scripting:Scripting
libraries:statistics") to statistics
```

Once you copy the file reference into "stastistics," you must "tell" AppleScript to use it. To take the average of a list of numbers, your script would look like this:

```
copy (load script file "Thendara:Scripting:Scripting
libraries:statistics") to statistics
tell statistics
    set listofNums to {2, 3, 4, 5}
    average()
end tell
```

Script objects give you a great deal of potential power. You can store subroutines in one script object and access them as necessary. You can set up these objects to do specific tasks and then access them whenever you need them.

## Networking with AppleScript

One of the most powerful aspects of AppleScript is its capability to send commands to programs running on other Macintoshes on a network. Although not very useful on a single machine, you may have a network at your office with several, or even hundreds of, Macintoshes. In that case, you could set up large projects that can take advantage of many different applications and data on many machines. You might use information in your accounting department's spreadsheets to look up information for your sales department, then write a letter about this specific information in a word processor on your assistant's machine, all from a script.

The possibilities for networked scripts are endless. You can upgrade software on other machines or back up key files from each person's machine every evening after closing. Entire projects can be distributed over a network to take advantage of every available machine.

Before you can start writing networked scripts, however, you have to do a small amount of set up.

## Network Setup

The capability to send Apple events over a network is closely tied to System 7's file sharing. It's not required, however, for you to share your hard drive, or even have file sharing on, to enable the feature necessary for scripts to take advantage of networked applications.

To enable a Macintosh to accept Apple events over a network, you must start its Program Linking, just as you must start File Sharing in order for people to access your hard drive across the network. To do this, open the Sharing Setup control panel. You'll see a section at the bottom that controls Program Linking. Unless you already have turned on this feature, the button will say "Start." Press it to make Program Linking available (see figure 9.1).

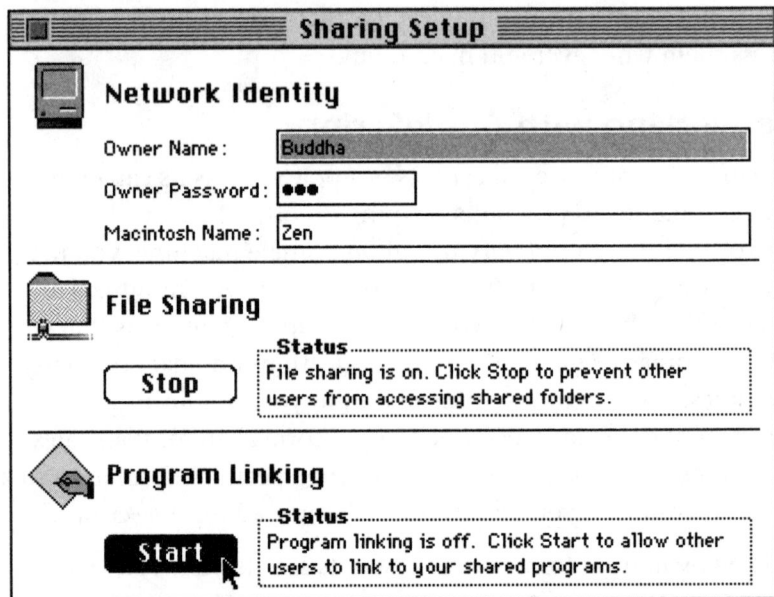

*Figure 9.1*
*The Sharing Setup control panel. Press the bottom button to turn Program Linking on and off.*

Just as you must specifically allow certain users to access your hard drive with file sharing, you must assign each user the privilege to send Apple events to your Mac over the network. To do this, go to the Users and Groups control panel, open on a user, and click the checkbox that allows that user to link to programs on your Macintosh (see figure 9.2). You must also assign yourself this privilege if you plan to use it.

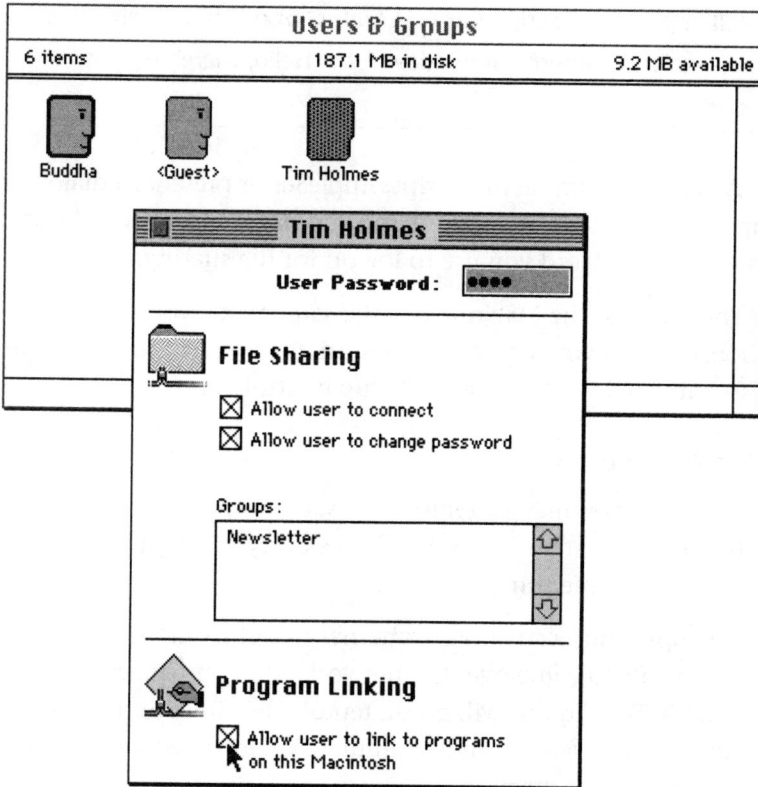

**Figure 9.2**
*You must specifically enable program linking for each user.*

Now that everything is set up, you can send some network scripts. Obviously, this works best if you have program linking privileges on another Mac on your network.

## Network Scripting

Sending a command to a networked application is not much different than sending a command to an application running on

179

your machine. You simply need to tell AppleScript where to find that application on the network.

To do this, you refer to an application *of* a particular machine *of* a particular zone (if you've got different zones on your network). For instance, to refer to the program "Scriptable Text Editor" on the machine named "Zen," you would write the following script:

```
tell application "Scriptable Text Editor" of machine "Zen"
    set the contents of window 1 to "Hello, there"
end tell
```

When you compile this script, AppleScript presents a dialog box that asks you to type in your name and password. This is the same name and password you use to log on for file sharing.

The name of the Macintosh is the same name you see in the Chooser when you log on to it. This name is stored in the Macintosh name field of the Sharing Setup control panel.

## Some Caveats

Although you may be tempted to set up every Mac on your network for Program Linking and give everyone privileges, you should keep some things in mind.

An application can choose whether or not to allow certain Apple events to come over the network. Many programs, such as Scriptable Text Editor, will give a remote user full control. As a result, the application can be completely controlled, just as if the user were on that machine.

Consider carefully whom you give these privileges. If you have private data, you may want to avoid giving Program Linking privileges to everyone who can connect to your Macintosh.

On the other hand, you can specify whether certain applications are accessible by Program Linking. Select the application in the Finder and choose "Sharing..." from the File menu (see figure 9.3). This will give you the option to disable Program Linking for that specific application.

*Figure 9.3*
*Choosing*
*Sharing... for a*
*program allows*
*you to disable*
*Program Linking*
*for that particular*
*application.*

Keep in mind that the Macintosh on the other end of the network doesn't need to have AppleScript installed. AppleScript already has translated the information into Apple events before it sends it to the remote application. As a result, you can control someone's copy of Scriptable Text Editor even if they don't have the AppleScript software running on their machine. This can be very useful for coordinating large projects. You need not worry about who's running AppleScript and who isn't. As long as the remote Macintosh is running the application that you want to control, everything will be fine.

Again, don't forget that you are giving someone else the capability to actually control an application on your Mac when you give them Program Linking privileges, so use common sense.

## Onward

You may be wondering where you should go from here, since you're now on your own in the scripting world. The next chapter will give you some direction for that question, so read on.

# *Spreading Your Wings*

One of the most important resources available when writing scripts is the dictionary of the application or scripting addition.

The dictionary stores information about every command and object that an application understands. Script Editor can easily access this information. Knowing how to interpret and efficiently use all the information in a dictionary may take some practice, but once you are accustomed to it you'll find dictionaries indispensable.

## Opening the Dictionary

To look at an application's dictionary use the Open Dictionary... command in Script Editor's File menu. Script Editor will present a directory dialog and ask you to choose a file to open. Only those files that have a dictionary within them will appear in this dialog.

Use the Open Dictionary... command and choose Scriptable Text Editor (see figure 10.1).

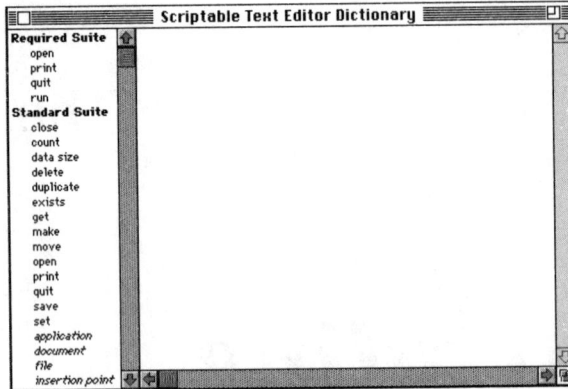

**Figure 10.1**
*The dictionary of Scriptable Text Editor opened in Script Editor.*

## How to Read the Dictionary

The dictionary window is divided into two parts. On the left is a list of all the commands and objects an application understands. This list is organized into suites—identified by large bold text. Commands are written in smaller text, while objects are italicized.

Clicking on a name in the list will display information about that command or object in the right side of the window. For instance, clicking on "make" in the list of commands under the heading "Standard Suite" will display information about the make command (see figure 10.2).

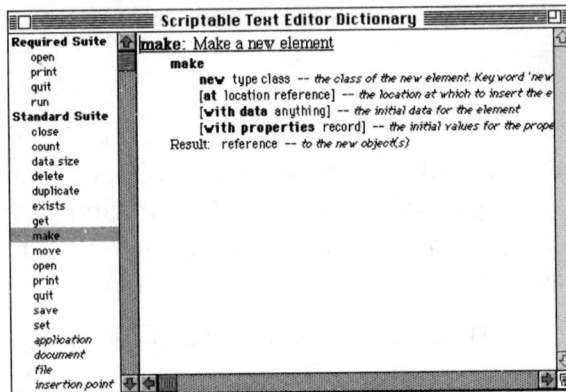

**Figure 10.2**
*The Dictionary shows information about the "make" command.*

# Looking Up Commands in the Dictionary

Script Editor gets the information about a command from the application. This information includes the name of the command, a short description of it, how to enter it into Script Editor, any parameters the command accepts, and the information it returns.

## Command Names and Descriptions

The information at the top is the command's name and a description of its function. When you click on "make" Script Editor shows you the name, "Make," and the description, "Make a new element."

Below the description is what must be typed into Script Editor to use the command. Any text presented in small bold type is the exact text which you must type as it appears in Script Editor to use the command (just as "make" is written on the second line).

## Objects of Commands

The second line may also contain information about the "direct object" of a command. This is the expression that would be placed immediately after the command. For example, clicking on the "set" command would show you that you must write "set" followed by a required reference (a path to an object).

Any lines that are indented and follow a command, describe parameters of that command. As you've learned, some commands have parameters that may be used to give more information about the command or to modify its behavior. Script Editor encloses optional parameters in brackets to differentiate them from required parameters. Parameters may occur in any order within a script.

Parameters are presented just as commands were—type the text into Script Editor first, followed by any necessary information, and finally what that information is and the function of the parameter.

## Command Data Descriptions

There are several standard descriptions of parameters and data that a command uses. You'll encounter these standard descriptions in an application's dictionaries. Here is a quick reference:

- reference—the path to an object, as in "word 1 of window 2 of application 'Scriptable Text Editor'"

- alias—a reference to a file, as in "file 'Thendara:Scripts:Sound Sucker'"

- anything—any valid data

- type class—the name of a particular object, as in "window" or "word"

- integer, text, real, record, list, boolean—indicates the use of a type of data

Other descriptions of the data abound, but most are fairly self-explanatory. The text following each description should be helpful as well.

Words divided by slashes are "constants" entered singly. For instance, the "close" command has the optional parameter "saving yes/no/ask." "yes/no/ask" is a choice you enter in the script after the "saving" command to tell Scriptable Text Editor what you want it to do. To close a window without saving the document, you would write:

```
close window 1 saving no
```

## Command Results

Dictionaries also describe information returned from a command. This information is put into the "result" variable.

## Looking Up Objects in the Dictionary

In addition to commands, the dictionary also contains information about objects that an application supports. These objects are italicized in the list on the left. To see an example of the available information about an object, click on the "word" object in the Scriptable Text Editor Suite (see figure 10.3).

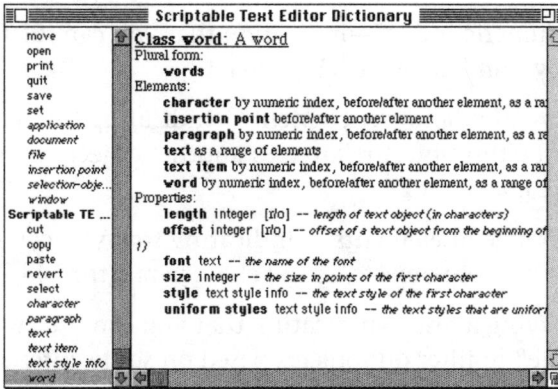

*Figure 10.3*
*The dictionary shows information about the word object.*

Script Editor provides information about the object, including what elements are contained within the object, and the properties of the object.

Just as it does for commands, the dictionary provides a description of the object in English terms. As you can see, the object "word" is described as "A word." This information is redundant in the case of an object so appropriately named, however you may encounter names that greatly benefit from these descriptions.

## Plurals

Immediately below the object description, the dictionary shows how to refer to that object as a plural, if applicable. For instance, if you wanted the first fourteen words, you would ask for "words 1 thru 14."

## Objects within Objects

Knowing what objects are contained in another object will help tremendously when you are trying to figure out how to refer to it. AppleScript lists these under the Elements heading.

Each of the objects listed under a parent object apply only to the parent object.

Following the name of each elemental object, the dictionary displays the different methods of referring to that object. For instance, you can refer to a character by the following methods:

- "by numeric index"—indicating that you can refer to characters by number, as in "character 1"

- "before/after another element"—indicating that you can describe this object relative to another object, as in "character before character 2"

- "as a range of elements"—indicating that you can refer to a range of these objects, as in "characters 1 thru 14"

- "satisfying a test"—indicating that you can use "whose" and "where" to filter out objects based on some criteria, as in "every character where it is 'f'"

Some objects also allow you to specify them "by name," as in "window 'untitled 1'." Though this is not the case for characters, you will see it for other objects.

## Object Properties

The dictionary lists information about the object properties you're interested in as well as the objects it contains under the Properties heading in the dictionary window.

Looking at these descriptions gives you a complete idea of how the properties are arranged. First is the name of the property. For example, words have a "length" property. Again, anything shown in small bold text is what you need to enter in your script to name that property. At the end of each property's line, you'll see a description of that property. For instance, the "length" property is "length of text object (in characters)."

## Object Value Data Types

Immediately after each property's name, the dictionary presents what kind of data represents the value of this property. In the case above, the length of word 1 is represented by an integer.

## Object Modification Ability

An object may have some modifiable properties. If the property can't be modified, the dictionary indicates this with the symbol "[r/o]" (for 'read only'). This means that you can't change the value of that property using a command, such as "set." However, you can still use a command like "get" to use the value of the property.

# Relating Commands to Objects

Knowing how to interpret information about commands and objects is only the first step in effectively using the dictionary. You must also understand how to combine commands and objects effectively when writing your scripts.

Remember, just because a command says that it works with a particular object, doesn't mean it will work with *all* objects. Unfortunately, there's no information in the dictionary to tell you which commands will work with an object. So how do you know?

The best way is to think about what the command does, and see if there's an intuitive action that the command would have on the particular object. For instance, consider the "close" command. It makes sense to use this with a "window" object. Intuitively, you can imagine what "closing" a "window" does. However, it doesn't make sense to "close" a "word." As a rule of thumb, if you can't easily imagine what using a command on a specific object will do, then that command probably won't work that way.

Sometimes, however, you can think of a way in which a command should work with an object, but won't. For instance, you might imagine that "getting" a window would result in the contents of that window being returned, just as "getting" a "word" returns the text of that word. Using "get" on a window results in an error—the only way to learn this is by trial and error.

As you create more and more scripts on your own, you'll find that you develop a "feel" for which commands will work with a particular object (or vice versa). All it takes is practice.

When you work with an application or scripting addition, you will find that the dictionary is an extremely valuable resource. It is compiled from the same information that AppleScript uses to get commands from a program, so you can be sure (barring the occasional programming error) that the commands you see in the dictionary are precisely what you need to enter into the script.

# On Your Own for Real

Congratulations! You've taken the last step toward independent scripting. You are now capable of creating almost any script. The next chapter and the following reference material have been created to help hone your skills with better organization and a more complete understanding of the specific commands built into AppleScript.

# The Road Goes Ever On

You've reached the end of your journey with us. As you crest this final hill you'll realize that your journey with AppleScript has really only begun.

We've shown you the basics of using AppleScript and writing scripts. However, these scripts have been based on ideas given to you. From now on you must come up with your own ideas and develop your own scripts.

I've come to love AppleScript in the year I've been using it. I come up with script ideas while walking down the street. Talking to users, I come up with ideas. Upon seeing new products, I immediately ask about AppleScript support. In short, AppleScript has become an obsession for me.

While I don't necessarily want you to become as obsessed as I have, I do hope that you can imagine a wealth of possibilities with AppleScript. We've gotten you started in this book by providing a few intriguing ways that AppleScript can be used, but hopefully you've come up with many more as you read and worked through these pages.

How you use AppleScript is up to you. Perhaps you have specific projects at work you'd like to automate, or utilities you'd like to write for your personal use, or perhaps you just want to play with it. No matter what you do with AppleScript, you are one of the people who will define what AppleScript becomes.

When this book was written, AppleScript was still a very new product. As this book was finished, AppleScript was recently released and Apple wasn't sure what to expect from this software. They have ideas about what people will be doing with it, but I think those views are too limited. Giving this kind of power to everyday users will result in an explosion of ideas and uses.

AppleScript is designed to be a means for generating custom solutions for your needs. If you have unique needs, it simply means that your solutions will be unique as well.

I'm excited about the future of AppleScript. I think users are extremely creative when using our Macs. I honestly believe that AppleScript is the single most useful utility you can have on your Mac.

And the best part is, AppleScript will continue to grow. Many developers are looking to implement AppleScript support into their own applications.

AppleScript places you at the center of a conglomerate of programs—able to pick and choose capabilities from each to achieve your goal. You no longer have to work within a single program's framework and be out of luck if the program doesn't meet your needs. With AppleScript support, a program can be tied into a script with several other programs to get the desired result.

It's an exciting time to use AppleScript, and I hope that you will use it to solve your particular needs. However, you shouldn't feel as though you are on your own. You can use many resources to expand your knowledge of AppleScript and your ideas for it. As the field expands, groups will form to exchange AppleScript ideas and information. New books will be written—focusing on specific aspects of using AppleScript in daily life. The AppleScript user will be able to draw from an unlimited number of sources.

## The Appendices

Though the main part of this book finishes with this chapter, there are several appendices for further aid. Appendix B is a complete guide to the native AppleScript language, including all the commands that come with the standard scripting additions. Many of these were discussed in the book itself, but you'll find commands that weren't covered—along with the exact phrasing in detail—as you flip through these pages.

Appendix A explains some of the technology behind the scenes. It describes the technical aspects of Apple events, how AppleScript gets information from an application's dictionary, and the Open Scripting Architecture.

You'll also find a glossary of potentially confusing terms, and a summary of the programs on the disk that came with the book.

## Groups

As of this pressing, I know of only one AppleScript Users Group. This is ADUA, the AppleScript Developers and Users Association. It is a meeting ground for users and developers, and provides a forum for exchanging ideas and opinions. Users can communicate their needs to developers, while developers can get new ideas for the kinds of support needed. Its goals are to promote AppleScript all across the Macintosh community and to set standards that will make using AppleScript easier for everyone.

You can get more information about ADUA by writing ADUA, 1814 Belmont Road N.W., Washington, D.C. 20009.

Many user groups have forums to discuss scripting issues. For example, BMUG's bulletin board, Planet BMUG, has a conference specifically devoted to scripting. You can use this conference to discuss scripting issues or questions, and even get technical support for this book.

Your local user group may have a conference on its BBS as well, or special interest groups that deal with scripting. Call your local user group to see what's available. This helps you find local people who are interested in discussing scripting and the things you want to do with it.

The national online services are another valuable source of information. People from all over the country discuss scripting issues in a common area. If you're a member of an online service, you may want to see what conferences meet your interests.

# Applications

Without applications, AppleScript is virtually useless. Though many programs are not yet scriptable via AppleScript, there are several available that will help you increase the amount of power and flexibility you can get from a script.

To help you get started, we've compiled a list of the products we feel are interesting and useful. This is by no means a complete list of programs that support AppleScript, but it's a start.

# Commercial Programs

Apple is pushing developers to include AppleScript support in their applications. As a result, more commercial programs that you buy will support AppleScript. Utilities, word processors, databases, graphics programs, and every other type of program might be scriptable in the near future.

If want to determine if a program is scriptable, call the company that manufactures it. If they say their program is not scriptable, tell them that you think it would be an extremely useful feature to have in the next version. Companies try to address the needs of their users. Remember to give good examples of how AppleScript support could really increase the productivity of the program.

To get you started, however, here are some of the programs we've used or enjoyed for their scriptability features.

# FileMaker Pro 2.0

We mentioned at the beginning of this book that BMUG has used this technology to automate the production of our 700-page disk catalog. One of the products that made this possible was FileMaker Pro 2.0. Not only is it a good database program, but it's fully scriptable. You can access any information stored in a database. The possibilities for this type of program are numerous, and FileMaker makes most of them plausible as well.

For instance, you can create a simple script that looks up a person's address when you select their name in your word processor, and then fills in that information, either in the letter you're writing or on a mailing label. Or you can create a script that uses information in your database to update your accounting software.

Contact Claris Corporation at 5201 Patrick Henry Drive, Santa Clara, CA, 95052-8618 (408) 727-8227.

# PageMaker 5.0

FileMaker Pro was only one part of the process that made our disk catalog automated. Equally important was the Apple event support in PageMaker 4.2. The new version has many improvements in the way the program works, and is definitely worth the upgrade.

Though it's only marginally scriptable, the presence of a thorough scripting language within PageMaker allows you to automate most aspects of the application. You can run commands in the native scripting language from AppleScript, and request every imaginable piece of information from the application.

Production people will find AppleScript to be very useful in augmenting their PageMaker use. Not only can you pull information from other applications and place into a layout, you can supplement PageMaker's own scripting language. Currently, PageMaker's built-in macro language can only perform a chain of commands. By using AppleScript and the ability to request information from the program, you can make truly intelligent scripts that manage your production work.

Contact Aldus, 411 First Ave. S, Suite 200, Seattle, WA, 98104, (206) 622-5500.

## Great Plains Accounting v6

This thorough accounting package is scriptable. You can access all the information in the software, allowing you to set up scripts that take advantage of the information.

You may want to couple this software with a database such as FileMaker Pro 2.0 to make a script that will get addresses for all the people that have outstanding balances with your company. You could look up their names in Great Plains, and then ask FileMaker for their addresses.

Contact Great Plains Software, 1701 SW 38th St., Fargo, ND, 58103, (800) 456-0025.

## Excel 4.0

Excel has been a long-standing giant in the Macintosh world. For years it was the only spreadsheet people used. Now, it's more powerful and includes AppleScript support. You can use AppleScript to get information from any cell in your spreadsheet and run Excel macros.

You could set up a script that retrieved information from a database program, use Excel to graph it, and place that graph into a document you were producing with PageMaker, all with the click of a button.

Contact Microsoft, One Microsoft Way, Redmond, WA, 98052-6399, (206) 882-8080.

## Microphone II v4.0.2

This has always been one of the leading telecommunications packages. It supports many different transfer protocols and terminal emulation. The latest version is somewhat scriptable. What it lacks in being scriptable by AppleScript, however, it makes up for in its own scripting language. You can use AppleScript to run a script stored in the Microphone document, and to get to set variables in those scripts.

You can do all sorts of things with this kind of ability, such as set up a database to store the electronic mail that you get from Microphone. Or you could set up a script that decompresses and virus-checks files downloaded by Microphone. Be sure you have version 4.0.2 or later, since previous versions had problems with their 'aete' resources.

Contact Software Ventures, 2907 Claremont Ave., Berkeley, CA, 94705, (510) 644-3232.

## SerePlot 2.0

SerePlot is a tool for scientific analysis, and it's one of the ideal programs for AppleScript support. If you are in a lab situation, you could use a data acquisition tool such as LabView, run a script that would take the data you acquired and run it through a set of steps with SerePlot. You could even set it up so that you never had to see the data, merely the analysis and graphs.

You could also set up an "intelligent" data processing script, that would look at the data you acquired, perhaps using Excel, and then do varying types of analysis based on how that data looks.

Contact Scientific Visions, PO Box 1971, Silver Spring, MD, 20915, (301) 593-0317.

## Scriptor

Do you find Script Editor limiting? As soon as you start doing intensive scripting, you'll quickly discover that Script Editor doesn't do some things that would make scripting much easier.

Scriptor may be the answer to your problems. It's a complete graphical environment for developing AppleScript scripts, and has all the features one would expect from an application designed to help you program. It allows you to step through a script one line at a time, watch variables change as the script runs, and quickly find errors you might not have anticipated.

It also gives you a graphical representation of a program's dictionary and enables you to build lines of script quickly and efficiently using that graphic dictionary. You don't have to type it in from scratch; Scriptor just asks for the information you need to enter and constructs the commands for you.

Contact Main Event Software, 1814 Belmont Road, N.W., Washington, D.C., 20009.

## Rosanne Utilities

This package of utilities is designed to give Macintosh users the capability to perform complex data processing quickly and easily. It provides an easy interface for setting up a process that analyzes large data files.

These applications are all scriptable and recordable. You could set up a process on a small data set and record your actions. When you were sure that the report came out the way you wanted, you could then run the script with a much larger data file.

You could use these applications as steps to create a large script that deals with complex data. You may use these utilities to get a file that represents a sampling of the data, and then feed that information to SerePlot for analysis.

If you work with large data files, or lots of small ones, these are the utilities you need.

Contact Main Event Software, 1814 Belmont Road, N.W., Washington, D.C., 20009.

## StuffIt Deluxe 3.0

We've included StuffIt Lite on the disk that comes with this book, but StuffIt Deluxe has many more capabilities. It's a full-featured utility for the compressing and archiving of data. It handles a wide variety of compression formats, is easy to use, and is our overall favorite compression utility.

Just like StuffIt Lite, it is fully scriptable and recordable. The latest version is even somewhat "attachable," allowing you to keep a list of scripts in the menu which can be run from within StuffIt Deluxe. Everything you can do from the user interface of StuffIt Deluxe 3.0 (and then some) you can do from a script.

You can use this capability to process files downloaded from online services: write a script that decompresses all the files in a particular folder and then sorts all the files into the appropriate places on your hard drive, putting After Dark modules into your After Dark Files folder, documentation into another folder, control panels into your Control Panels folder, etc.

Alternatively, you could use StuffIt Deluxe in a script that backs up files on your hard drive, compressing the files before moving them to your backup volume.

Contact Aladdin Systems, 165 Westridge Dr., Watsonville, CA, 95076, (408) 761-6200.

## QuicKeys

QuicKeys is easily the most popular macro utility on the Macintosh. It has the capability to record actions in any application and play them back for you.

QuicKeys can now be controlled by AppleScript, and QuicKeys can run AppleScript scripts. This makes the two able to communicate with one another quickly and easily. The two programs are perfect complements. AppleScript can't control dialogs or menus, but QuicKeys can. So, if you do something from a script which generates a dialog, you can run a QuicKey to deal with that dialog, allowing your script to continue uninterrupted.

Another reason for using QuicKeys is that AppleScript can only control applications that are AppleScript-aware. QuicKeys, on the other hand, doesn't require this.

QuicKeys, however, doesn't currently provide any sort of language capability. AppleScript can provide this, allowing you to execute different QuicKey sequences based on information you get from a program.

Contact CE Software, P.O. Box 65580, West Des Moines, IA, 50265, (515) 224-1995.

## Mirror

One of AppleScript's biggest problems is a lack of interface. Though you can put up simple dialogs, and more complex ones with DialogRunner, you can't create a fully-featured interface such as the one you're used to in Mac applications.

Mirror is the code name for a product that is being developed to solve this problem. It provides a complete set of tools for designing an interface in which to run your scripts. They can have a complete front end and each item in that interface can have a script attached to it. Users of HyperCard may recognize this program's ancestors, WindowScript and Dialoger.

In addition to enabling you to add any interface element you can think of, Mirror has the capability to make stand-alone applications to carry the interface elements with them. You can give your script to a friend and he does not need Mirror to see the interface.

This program is very cool, easy to use, and quite powerful. The company intends to finish the product in September, but they're not making any guarantees.

Contact Heizer Software, P.O. Box 232019, Pleasant Hill, CA, 94523, (800) 888-7667.

## Picture Press 2.5

This is a picture compression utility that works with a wide variety of formats. It's thoroughly scriptable, enabling you to manipulate pictures and obtain information about them all from a script. One suggestion the authors have is to set up a folder to be watched by a utility like Folder Watcher, and to compress any picture files placed into it.

Contact Storm Technology, 1861 Landings Dr., Mountain View, CA, 94043, (415) 691-6600.

## Frontier

On some levels, Frontier is a competing product to AppleScript. It too provides a scripting language that can control Apple events. The similarity is only superficial though, as Frontier has the capability to do more than control Apple events. It contains a word processor, an outliner, and a database. In addition, it's a powerful file processing utility. All of its functionality is completely scriptable with a very powerful scripting language.

If you're interested in going further with scripting, you should take a look at UserLand's Frontier. Future versions of Frontier will be accessible through the Open Scripting Architecture, allowing you to access the powerful Frontier scripting language as easily as you can AppleScript. In addition, future versions may allow you to edit AppleScript scripts in the Frontier environment.

Contact Userland Software, 400 Seaport Ct., Redwood City, CA, 94063, (415) 369-6600.

## Publicly Distributable Software

While there are many commercial applications that support AppleScript, this is also accomplished by several publicly-distributed programs. As the market for AppleScript grows, th is support will spread. If you have access to an online service or local BBS, check for the programs listed below.

If you don't have access to one of these services, try calling your local user group (or BMUG) and see if they have these files in their library.

## Shaman

Shaman, short for sharing manager, is an application for managing file sharing. It displays the status of file sharing via an icon in the menu bar, and enables you to quickly and easily start and stop file sharing. It is scriptable and recordable, so you can set up scripts that utilize these features.

Contact Robert Hess, at robert_hess@macweek.ziff.com.

## EasyPlay 1.0

EasyPlay is a very powerful QuickTime utility. It features an extensive dictionary and is fully scriptable. You can set up scripts that play movies, catalog them, or anything else you can do from within the application.

Contact Leptonic Systems Inc., at 76004.1447@compuserve.com.

## Folder Watcher 2.0.1

This is a Shareware application that enables you to "watch" folders on your hard drive or across the network. Any time the contents of a watched folder changes, Folder Watcher can log the change, play a sound, show a dialog, and/or run a script. For example, you can use this to watch an "In Box" folder and run a script that decompresses any compressed files in that folder and organizes them on your hard drive. Or you could write a script to synchronize folders across a network, ensuring that the contents of the two folders are the same on both machines. This is included on the disk.

Contact Joe Zobkiw, at aflzobkiw@aol.com.

## StuffIt Lite

One of the most popular compression/decompression utilities in the Shareware industry, StuffIt Lite is extremely powerful. For the small $25 Shareware fee, you can become a registered user. It's a great deal.

Check it out! It's included on the disk.

Contact Aladdin Systems, at aladdin@aol.com.

# *Behind the Scenes*

By now you should be familiar with what goes on with a script once it's written. You may be curious, however, about what's going on "under the hood" to make that script work. This section gives you a brief description of each of the key aspects.

## Apple Events

The core technology behind AppleScript is "Apple events." Introduced as part of System 7, Apple events enables two programs to communicate directly with one another.

An Apple event is a message sent from the "client" application, such as AppleScript, that tells the "server" application, such as Scriptable Text Editor, to perform a specific action. An Apple event can do more than simply command an application. It also can send data to that application and ask for data from it.

An Apple event is composed of three parts: a destination application, the command or event, and the data to be sent.

## Specifing the Server

Quill was the
name of
Scriptable Text
Editor in the pre-
release version of
AppleScript.

There are several ways to point to an application with Apple events. The most common is to use the creator signature of the destination application. The System software uses this unique four-letter code to track which application a document belongs to. To send an Apple event to Scriptable Text Editor, you would address it to the program with the signature "quil."

## Specifing the Event

An event is made up of two parts: the class and the ID. Four-letter codes represent these parts. The class of an AppleEvent represents the group (or "suite") of Apple events that the event is found in. The ID of an Apple event is a unique identifier of that specific command in that group. For instance, the "get data" event (which the "get" command sends) is in the Apple event class "core" and its ID is "getd."

Apple has defined four categories of Apple event suites that a program can potentially support: Required, Core, Functional-area, and Custom.

Required events are those which an application must support in order to work efficiently with the System software. These events are Open Application, which is sent to a program to start it; Open Documents, which tells an application to open a set of documents; Print Documents, which tells an application to print a set of documents; and Quit, which quits an application. A program doesn't *need* to support these events, but Apple strongly recommends that they do.

Core events are commands that every program should support for easy, intuitive communication. Some examples of core events are Get Data, Set Data, Count Elements, and Create Elements.

Functional-area events are suites of events with similar functionality. For instance, all events that deal with manipulating text are contained within the Text suite; while those that deal with database manipulation are in the Database suite.

Custom events are those defined to deal with information specific to an application. For instance, StuffIt 3.0 has a suite of events that deals with archive manipulation, and the System 7 Finder takes a series of events that are relevant to Finder actions. A developer can choose to keep their events suites private or publish their events, so that others can use them.

## Specifing the Data

The data portion of an Apple event is organized into parameters, with each described by a keyword. A parameter of the Get Data event is the specific object you wish to get. This parameter is identified by a keyword; another four-letter code, that says "get the following data." This is followed by codes that describe the actual data. For example, "word 3 of window 1 of application Scriptable Text Editor." The actual data would look something like: {----,cwrd,indx,3,cwnd,indx,1,capl,pnam,"Scriptable Text Editor"}. This sample of the data structure of an Apple event is a good example of why AppleScript is a more effective way to use Apple events then executing them directly.

## AppleScript Sleight of Hand

Now that you have an idea of how Apple events work, you may be wondering how AppleScript translates a typical Apple event into an easy-to-use command that can be used from Script Editor.

Actually, AppleScript doesn't. The program receiving the Apple event provides the English equivalent of the command to AppleScript. Scriptable applications have an 'aete' resource (for Apple Event Terminology Extension). This resource is a list of all the events that program can understand, along with their English equivalents.

When AppleScript first compiles commands for an application, it reads in this information. AppleScript then knows the corresponding events to send that application when you use those commands to run a script.

Using the "Open Dictionary…" command in Script Editor enables you to look at the 'aete' resource. Script Editor formats the information so it's more easily understood.

This resource also contains information about the objects the application understands, the English equivalent of that object, other objects contained within it, and its properties.

## The Open Scripting Architecture

While Apple has built an easy-to-use scripting language and an event mechanism, they've also created a framework for allowing others to create their own system-level scripting languages. This is called the Open Scripting Architecture (OSA). AppleScript is merely the first language to take advantage of it.

Any OSA-aware scripting language can be used from within Script Editor as long as the component for that language is in your Extensions folder. The AppleScript file now in your Extensions folder is such a component.

Once installed, a scripting language can take advantage of the 'aete' resources in your applications and the scripting additions in your Scripting Additions folder. In the lower left corner of the Script Editor window, there is a box with the word AppleScript in it. Clicking in that box reveals that it is actually a pop-up menu that enables you to select among multiple scripting languages (although only AppleScript is currently present).

Why would you want to switch from AppleScript to another language? Other languages may give you more powerful logic or formatting capabilities than AppleScript. As the OSA becomes more widely installed there will be more and more ways to use the technology underlying AppleScript.

## Interapplications Communications

Those are the basics behind Apple events, AppleScript, and OSA. There are more advanced aspects to how they function, however that is beyond the scope of this book. If interested, you should look at the *Interapplication Communications* volume of the *Inside Macintosh* series. It is designed for programmers, so it's not what one might consider pleasure reading. Nevertheless, it contains all the information you can ever want on Apple events.

## Onward

This technology is extremely flexible. From new languages with strange and unique capabilities to applications that rely completely on other applications to function.

Who knows, you may be the one of the people who creates them!

# *Rules of the Road*

Many of the AppleScript commands have been covered in the preceding chapters. However, many more have not. This appendix covers commands briefly to help you utilize them. It is divided into two sections: the actions of the AppleScript language, and its built-in variables.

This section uses certain typographical conventions to explain the commands. Here's a summary of those notations:

- Plain text indicates text that you enter directly into the script area

- Italicized text indicates a value that you must enter each time you use that value

- Text within brackets indicates an optional parameter

- Text separated by vertical bars indicates several options in a list, any of which could be used

# Commands, Symbols, and Similar Mechanisms

## & (ampersand)

WHAT IT DOES     Concatenates two strings, two lists, or a list and some other piece of data.

SYNTAX     *string1* & *string2*

*list1* & *list2*

*list1* & *anyData*

RESULT     Returns the new string, or list, that arises from the concatenation.

NOTES     If you use the & symbol with two strings, AppleScript combines the two strings into one long string. If you use this symbol with two lists, AppleScript makes one long list where all the items from the left list are put first and all the items from the second list are put at the end.

If you use the & symbol with a list and any other piece of data, AppleScript puts the piece of data into the list as a new item in the list.

EXAMPLE     This following script puts {3, 4, 5, 6} into the result window:

---

{3, 4, 5} & 6

---

## * (multiplication)

WHAT IT DOES     Multiplies two numbers together.

SYNTAX        *number1\*number2*

RESULT        Returns the product of *number1* and *number2*.

NOTES         In a mathematical expression with several operators, multiplication and division are performed first, from left to right, after AppleScript evaluates any parenthetical statements and after it applies all negations.

EXAMPLE       This script puts 42 into the result window:

---
6 * 7
---

SEE ALSO      ÷, +, -, ^, *mod, div*

## + (addition)

WHAT IT DOES      Adds two numbers together.

SYNTAX      *number1+number2*

RESULT      Returns the sum of *number1* and *number2*.

NOTES      When running a mathematical expression that uses several mathematical operators, addition is performed left to right after multiplication, division, negation, and parenthetical statements.

EXAMPLE      This script puts 6 into the result window:

---
3 + 3
---

SEE ALSO      -, *, ÷, ^, *mod, div*

## - (subtraction)

WHAT IT DOES    Subtracts one number from another, or changes the sign of a number.

SYNTAX    *number1-number2*

*-number*

RESULT    If subtracting two numbers, this operator returns the difference between the two numbers, subtracting the right number from the left number. If changing the sign of a number, this operator returns the number with its sign changed.

NOTES    When working with a mathematical expression that contains many operators, this operator is handled differently depending on its instant use. If being used for subtraction, it's performed at the same time as addition—after multiplication and division, negation, and parenthetical statements. If used to change the sign of a number, it is performed before operators, except statements in parentheses.

EXAMPLE    This script puts 2 into the result window:

```
5 - 3
```

This script puts -2 into the result window:

```
-2
```

SEE ALSO    +, *, ÷, *mod, div*

## < (less than)

WHAT IT DOES    Determines if one expression is less than another.

SYNTAX     *expression1 < expression2*

RESULT     Returns true if *expression1* is less than *expression2*; returns false if it is not.

NOTES     The expressions can be any one of the following:

Dates: If you have two dates, AppleScript considers one less than another if it comes before the other chronologically.

Integers and Real numbers: Real numbers are those with a decimal component; integers don't have decimals attached to them. AppleScript can compare two integers or two real numbers to determine which one is less than the other.

Strings: AppleScript considers a string that comes first alphabetically to be less than another.

You can only compare two expressions that are of the same type, such as strings to strings and dates to dates. If you compare an integer to a real number, AppleScript will coerce the integer value to a real number and then decide which value is smaller.

This symbol can be replaced by several equivalent phrases:

*expression1* is less than *expression2*

*expression1* comes before *expression2*

*expression1* is not greater than or equal to *expression2*

EXAMPLE     This script puts true into the result window:

---

3 < 4

---

SEE ALSO     >, ≤, ≥, =, ≠

## > (greater than)

WHAT IT DOES     Determines if one expression is greater than another.

SYNTAX     *expression1 > expression2*

RESULT     Returns true if *expression1* is greater than *expression2*; returns false if it is not.

NOTES        The expressions can be any one of the following:

Dates: If you have two strings in AppleScript date format, AppleScript thinks one is greater than the other if it comes after the other chronologically.

Integers and Real numbers: Real numbers are those with a decimal component; integers don't have decimals attached to them. AppleScript can compare two integers or two real numbers to determine which is greater than the other.

Strings: AppleScript considers a string that comes later alphabetically to be greater than another.

You can only compare two expressions that are of the same type, such as strings to strings and dates to dates. If you compare an integer to a real number, AppleScript will coerce the integer value to a real number and then decide which value is larger.

This symbol can be replaced by several equivalent phrases:

*expression1* is greater than *expression2*

*expression1* comes after *expression2*

*expression1* is not less than or equal to *expression2*

EXAMPLE      This script puts true into the result window:

---

4 > 3

---

SEE ALSO     <, ≥, ≤, =, ≠

## = (equal to)

WHAT IT DOES     Determines if two expressions are equal to one another.

SYNTAX          *expression1* = *expression2*

RESULT          Returns true if *expression1* is equal to *expression2*; returns false if it is not.

| | |
|---|---|
| NOTES | *expression1* and *expression2* can be any valid AppleScript expression, including variables or data from other applications. |
| | This symbol also can be replaced by several equivalent phrases: |
| | *expression1* is *expression2* |
| | *expression1* is equal to *expression2* |
| | *expression1* equals *expression2* |
| | *expression1* equal *expression2* |
| | *expression1* equal to *expression2* |
| EXAMPLE | This script puts true into the result window: |

"The Tao of AppleScript" = "The Tao of AppleScript"

| | |
|---|---|
| SEE ALSO | ≠, >, <, ≤, ≥ |

## ^ (caret)

| | |
|---|---|
| WHAT IT DOES | Raises one number to the power of another. |
| SYNTAX | *number1^number2* |
| RESULT | Returns the result of raising *number1* to the power of *number2*. |
| NOTES | When using a mathematical expression that contains many operators, "to the power of" is performed after negation, division, and before addition and subtraction. |
| EXAMPLE | This script puts 81 (9 squared) into the result window: |

9 ^ 2

| | |
|---|---|
| SEE ALSO | *, ÷, +, -, *mod*, *div* |

## ≠ (not equal to)

| | |
|---|---|
| WHAT IT DOES | Determines if one expression is not equal to another. |
| SYNTAX | *expression1 ≠ expression2* |
| RESULT | Returns true if *expression1* does not equal *expression2*; returns false if it does. |
| NOTES | This symbol can be replaced with a number of equivalent phrases: |

*expression1* is not *expression2*

*expression1* isn't *expression2* (AppleScript expands this to "is not" when it compiles)

*expression1* is not equal to *expression2* (or the contraction "isn't")

*expression1* does not equal *expression2* (Again, you can use the contraction "doesn't" which will be expanded upon compiling.)

This symbol is made by typing Option-=.

| | |
|---|---|
| EXAMPLE | This script puts true into the result window, because 5 is not equal to 3: |

---

5 ≠ 3

---

| | |
|---|---|
| SEE ALSO | =, ≤, ≥, <, > |

## ≤ (less than or equal to)

| | |
|---|---|
| WHAT IT DOES | Determines if one expression is less than or equal to another. |
| SYNTAX | *expression1 ≤ expression2* |
| RESULT | Returns true if *expression1* is less than or equal to *expression2*; returns false if it is not. |
| NOTES | The expressions can be any one of the following: |

Dates: If you have two dates, AppleScript considers one less than the other if it comes first chronologically.

Integers and Real numbers: Real numbers are those with a decimal component; integers don't have decimals attached to them. AppleScript can compare two integers or two real numbers to determine which is less than the other.

Strings: AppleScript considers one string less than another if it comes first alphabetically.

You can compare only two expressions that are of the same type, such as strings to strings and dates to dates. If you compare an integer to a real number, AppleScript will coerce the integer value to a real number and then decide which is less.

This symbol can be replaced by several equivalent phrases:

*expression1 <= expression2*

*expression1* is less than or equal to *expression2*

*expression1* does not come after *expression2*

*expression1* less than or equal to *expression2*

This symbol is made by typing Option-comma.

EXAMPLE    This script puts true into the result window:

---

3 ≤ 4

---

SEE ALSO    ≥, <, ≤, =, ≠

## ≥ (greater than or equal to)

WHAT IT DOES    Determines if one expression is greater than or equal to another.

SYNTAX    *expression1 ≥ expression2*

RESULT    Returns true if *expression1* is greater than or equal to *expression2*; returns false if it is not.

NOTES    The expressions can be any one of the following:

Dates: If you have two dates, AppleScript considers one greater than the other if it comes first chronologically.

Integers and Real numbers: Real numbers are those with a decimal component; integers don't have decimals attached to them. AppleScript can compare two integers or two real numbers to determine which is less than the other.

Strings: AppleScript considers one string greater than another if it comes after the other string alphabetically.

You can compare only two expressions that are of the same type, such as strings to strings and dates to dates. If you compare an integer to a real number, AppleScript will coerce the integer value to a real number and then decide which is greater.

This symbol can be replaced by several equivalent phrases:

*expression1* >= *expression2*

*expression1* is greater than or equal to *expression2*

*expression1* does not come before *expression2*

*expression1* greater than or equal to *expression2*

This symbol is made by typing Option-Period.

EXAMPLE    This script puts true into the result window:

---

4 ≥ 3

---

SEE ALSO    ≤, <, >, =, ≠

## ÷ (division)

WHAT IT DOES    Divides one number by another.

SYNTAX    *number1 ÷ number2*

RESULT    Returns the quotient of the two numbers, dividing *number1* by *number2*.

NOTES     When using a mathematical expression that contains many operators, division is performed at the same time as multiplication, immediately after negation and parenthetical statements.

This operator always returns a real number with a decimal component, as in 3.0.

This symbol is made by typing Option-/.

You also can use the "/" character when writing a script, and AppleScript will replace it with the symbol "÷".

EXAMPLE     This script puts .5 into the result window:

---

```
3 ÷ 6
```

---

SEE ALSO     *, *mod, div, ^, +*

## a reference to

WHAT IT DOES     Forces AppleScript to set a variable to the path of an object, rather than the value of that object itself.

SYNTAX     a reference to *an objectPath*

RESULT     Returns the path to the object that you specify in *objectPath*.

EXAMPLE     The following script puts "The" into the result window:

---

**set** x **to a reference to** word 1 **of** window 1 **of** application "Scriptable Text Editor"

**set the** contents **of** window 1 **of** application "Scriptable Text Editor" **to** "The Tao of AppleScript"

**get** x

---

## activate

WHAT IT DOES     The activate command brings an application to the front. This is equivalent to choosing the application in the application menu.

SYNTAX  activate application *appName*

tell application *appName* to activate

tell application *appName*

[commands]

activate

[commands]

end tell

RESULT  Brings the specified application to the front.

NOTES  The activate scripting addition is stored directly within the AppleScript extension. You should be aware that if you "activate" the Finder it will cause your Mac to hang.

EXAMPLE  This script brings the application Scriptable Text Editor to the front:

activate application "Scriptable Text Editor"

## and

WHAT IT DOES  Determines if two Boolean values are true.

SYNTAX  *boolean1* and *boolean2*

RESULT  Returns true if both *boolean1* and *boolean2* are true; returns false if either is false.

NOTES  *boolean1* and *boolean2* can be any AppleScript expression that produces a Boolean value, such as "x = 4" or "true."

Each Boolean must be placed in parentheses.

If AppleScript sees that the first Boolean is false, it won't check the second.

EXAMPLE  This script puts true into the result window because both expressions return a Boolean value of true.

---

**copy** 3 **to** x

(x = 3) **and** (true)

---

SEE ALSO    or, not

## as

WHAT IT DOES    Coerces a value to another type of data.

SYNTAX    *expression* as *dataType*

RESULT    Forces AppleScript to look at the information in *expression* as if were another type of data that is specified in *dataType*, such as treating numbers as strings. Returns the new value after it was coerced.

NOTES    For most occasions, you need not worry about coercing the data; AppleScript will take care of it for you.

EXAMPLE    This script puts the string "1" into the result window:

---

1 **as** string

---

## ASCII character

WHAT IT DOES    Given a number from 0 to 255, AppleScript converts that number to a character based on the ASCII standard for representing characters by numbers.

SYNTAX    ASCII character [of] *integer*

RESULT    Returns the ASCII character represented by an *integer*.

NOTES    This command is stored in a scripting addition named "String Commands."

ASCII is a standard method of referring to characters by assigning them numbers. ASCII only applies to standard text, so the characters you get by using the Option key on a Macintosh are not available.

Some commonly used ASCII codes are

13 (Return or Control-M)

14 (line feed or Control-N)

32 (Space)

9 (Tab or Control-I)

EXAMPLE      This script puts a space character in the result window:

---

ASCII character of 32

---

SEE ALSO      *ASCII number*

## ASCII number

WHAT IT DOES      Given a character in the ASCII character set, this command returns the number for that character.

SYNTAX      ASCII number [of] *character*

RESULT      Returns the number associated with the character you typed, using the ASCII standards.

NOTES      This command is stored in a scripting addition named "String Commands."

ASCII is a standard method of referring to characters by assigning them numbers. ASCII only applies to standard text, so the characters you get from using the Option key on a Macintosh are not available.

EXAMPLE      This script puts the number 65 into the result window:

---

ASCII number of "A"

---

SEE ALSO      *ASCII character*

## beep

WHAT IT DOES      Beeps one time, or a specified number of times, using the current System beep and volume.

SYNTAX     beep [*number*]

RESULT     The Macintosh beeps once with no parameter, or the number of times you specify.

NOTES      This command is stored in a scripting addition named "Beep."

EXAMPLE    This script beeps three times:

---

beep 3

---

## choose application

WHAT IT DOES    Displays a dialog box for choosing a running application to which it sends commands. This dialog lists applications on the same machine as the script and on networked machines (see below).

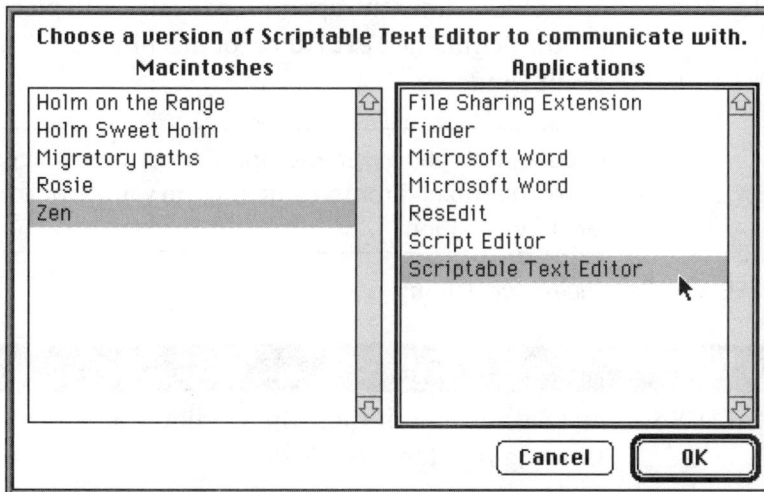

---

**Choose a version of Scriptable Text Editor to communicate with.**

| Macintoshes | Applications |
|---|---|
| Holm on the Range | File Sharing Extension |
| Holm Sweet Holm | Finder |
| Migratory paths | Microsoft Word |
| Rosie | Microsoft Word |
| Zen | ResEdit |
| | Script Editor |
| | Scriptable Text Editor |

[ Cancel ]   [ OK ]

---

SYNTAX     choose application [with prompt *string*] [application label *string*]

RESULT     The Macintosh displays the dialog. If you use the "with prompt *string*" parameter, the dialog will use the string at the top of the window. If you use the "label *string*" parameter, the dialog will have a text string over the list of applications. The command returns the network address of the chosen application to the script.

If the user presses the "Cancel" button in the dialog, it stops the script, unless the command is part of a "try" statement.

NOTES    You write the network address of an application as follows:

application *appName* of machine *macName* of zone *zoneName*

where *appName* is the name of the application, *macName* is the name of the Macintosh on the network where that application is running; *zoneName* is the name of the zone where that Macintosh is located.

If you and the Macintosh are in the same zone, "of zone *zoneName*" can be excluded from the network address.

EXAMPLE    This script shows the appropriate dialog and places "application 'Scriptable Text Editor' of machine 'Zen'" into the result window:

---

choose application with prompt "Choose a version of Scriptable Text Editor to communicate with." application label "Applications"

---

SEE ALSO    *choose file, tell, try*

## choose file

WHAT IT DOES    Enables the user of the script to choose a particular file by showing the standard file dialog.

SYNTAX    choose file [with prompt *string*] [of type *listOfTypes*]

RESULT    Shows a standard file dialog with the prompt you specified in the "with prompt *string*" parameter. Using the "of type *listOfTypes*" parameter enables you to show only files of certain types that are specified in a list.

NOTES     The command returns the path of the file that was selected, in the following format:

alias "Disk:Folder:Folder:File"

This result does not have to be described as a file path
(using "file"), since AppleScript already recognizes this as a
file path.

If the user presses the "Cancel" button in the dialog, it
stops the script, unless the command is part of a "try"
statement.

EXAMPLE     This script displays a dialog that enables the user to select
only "TEXT" and "PICT" files, and then places the file
path of the selected file into the result window:

```
choose file with prompt "Choose a file to open with
TeachText." of type {"TEXT", "PICT"}
```

SEE ALSO     *choose application, info for*

## considering

WHAT IT DOES     Enables you to consider certain attributes for comparing
two strings.

SYNTAX     considering *attribute1*[, *attribute2* ,..., and *attribute5*] [but
ignoring *attribute1*[,*attribute2*,..., and *attribute5*]]

         *commands*

end considering

RESULT     When considering an attribute, AppleScript takes that
attribute into account when comparing the two strings.

NOTES     Possible attributes are shown in the following table.

EXAMPLE     The following script puts false into the result window,
because when considering the case of the two strings,
"ABC" is not in "abcdef":

---

considering case
   "ABC" **is contained by** "abcdef"
**end considering**

---

SEE ALSO   *ignoring*

## contains

WHAT IT DOES   Determines if one string, list, or record contains another.

SYNTAX   *string1|list1|record1* contains *string2|list2|record2*

RESULT   Returns true if the value on the right is contained within the value on the left.

NOTES   When comparing lists, a list only contains another list if all the items in the second list are contained in the first in the same order.

When comparing records, one record contains another if all the labels are the same and the values for each label are the same.

EXAMPLE   This script puts true into the result window:

---

"The Tao of AppleScript" **contains** "e Ta"

---

SEE ALSO   *=, ≠, is contained by, is not contained by, starts with, ends with, does not contain*

## copy

WHAT IT DOES   Copies data to a variable, or to the value of an object, in an application.

SYNTAX   copy *data* to *variableName*

copy *data* to *objectPath*

RESULT   Puts the data into the variable *variableName* or into the object you specified with *objectPath*. This data is also put into the result.

NOTES     This command actually makes a copy of the data. This may cause memory problems when working with large lists or records. The "set" command can alleviate some of this burden.

If you copy a piece of information out of an application, this is equivalent to using the get command and then using the result of that command.

EXAMPLE     This script puts the number 3 into the variable named x and the result window:

---

**copy** 3 **to** x

---

This script copies "the" to the first word of the first window in Scriptable Text Editor:

---

**copy** "The" **to** word 1 **of** window 1 **of** application "Scriptable Text Editor"

---

SEE ALSO     *set, get*

## count

WHAT IT DOES     Counts the number of items in a group of items.

SYNTAX     count [of] *pluralItem* [each *typeOfItem*]

RESULT     Counts the number of items in a set.

NOTES     Although you can use this command to count the objects contained in some other object, you can do this only if the application supports that Apple Event. To find out if it does, use "Open Dictionary..." from Script Editor to look for a "count" command.

You also can use the phrase "number of" in place of count. For example, "number of words in "The Tao of AppleScript."

EXAMPLE     This script puts 3 into the result window:

---

count items of {"The","Tao of","AppleScript"}

---

This script puts 4 into the result window:

---

count words in "The Tao of AppleScript"

---

This script puts 5 into the result window ("four" is a string, not an integer):

---

count {1, 2, 3, "four", 5, 6} each integer

---

## current date

| | |
|---|---|
| WHAT IT DOES | Returns the current date and time. |
| SYNTAX | current date |
| RESULT | Returns the current date and time in AppleScript's date format. The result will look something like "date 'April 26,1993 10:26:05 PM'." |
| NOTES | This command comes from a scripting addition named "Current Date." |
| | The "date" tells AppleScript that it should consider this as a date, much as "file" tells AppleScript to interpret a string as a file path. This means that the string can be handled as a date, and therefore used in comparisons. |
| EXAMPLE | This script puts the current date and time into the result window: |

---

current date

---

| | |
|---|---|
| SEE ALSO | <, >, ≤, ≥ |

## display dialog

| | |
|---|---|
| WHAT IT DOES | Builds a dialog with the elements you specify, then returns information about what happened in the dialog. |

SYNTAX    display dialog *promptstring* [default answer *answerString*]
[buttons *listOfButtons*] [defaultbutton*buttonNumber*
|*buttonName*] [with icon*iconNumber*|caution|stop|notify]

RESULT    Shows a dialog with the parameters you specify, where
*promptString* is the text that appears in the dialog as the
prompt. When using the "default answer *answerString*"
parameter, AppleScript puts one editable text field in the
window, with the contents of that field set to the value in
*answerString*. When using the "buttons *listOfButtons*"
parameter, AppleScript enables you to name and place up
to three buttons in the dialog box, where *listOfButtons* is a
list containing the names of the buttons. Using the "default button" parameter enables you to specify which
button you press when you press the Return key. The
default button can be specified by either its number in the
dialog, or by the text within the button. Using the "with
icon" parameter, AppleScript puts an icon in the dialog.
You can specify the icon by its resource ID number, and
you can use any icon that is in the script file, the current
application in a "tell" statement, or in the System file. You
also can use the built-in icons "stop," "notify," or "cau-
tion," that are found in the System file.

The information about what happened in the dialog is
returned in a record. The "text returned" label contains the
text that was typed into the dialog's editable text field. The
"button returned" label contains the name of the button
that was pressed to dismiss the dialog.

NOTES    The "number" of a button is its placement in the dialog. If
you used a list of your own buttons, item 1 of the list is the
first item, item 2 the second, and so on. Otherwise, the
"OK" button is number 1 and the "Cancel" button is
number 2.

AppleScript's dialogs enable you to press Return or Enter to
dismiss the dialog, as if you had pressed the OK button,
and Escape or Command-period to dismiss the dialog with
the Cancel button.

If you want the editable text field to be blank when the dialog first appears, write "" for the *answerString*.

Pressing the Cancel button also returns an error that you can use with the "try" statement.

This command is stored in a scripting addition named "Display Dialog."

EXAMPLE    This script shows a dialog that uses all the available options, and then puts the returned record into the result window:

---

display dialog "Your hard drive will be erased if you do not enter the correct password!" default answer "" buttons {"No", "Maybe later", "Cancel"} default button "Maybe later" with icon stop

---

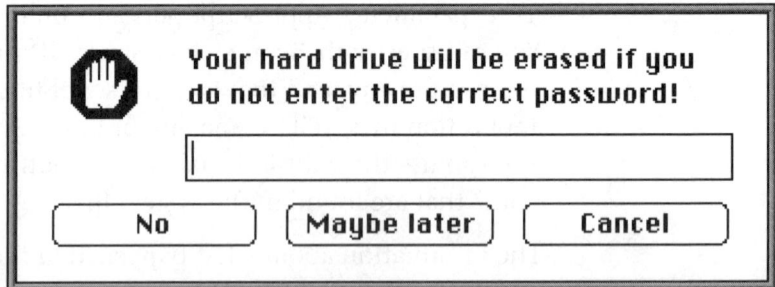

## div

WHAT IT DOES    Divides one number by the other, but only returns the integer portion of the answer.

SYNTAX    *number1* div *number2*

RESULT    Returns the integer portion of the quotient of *number1* and *number2*.

NOTES    When used in a mathematical expression with several operators, div is performed at the same time as other division.

EXAMPLE | This script puts 1 into the result window:

**5 div** 3

SEE ALSO | *mod, ÷, \*, -, +, ^, round*

## does not contain

WHAT IT DOES | Determines if one value does not contain another value.

SYNTAX | *string1|list1|record1* does not contain *string2|list2|record2*

RESULT | Returns true if the first item does not contain the second item.

NOTES | When comparing lists, a list contains another list if all the items in the second list are contained in the first in the same order.

When comparing records, one record contains another if all the labels are the same and the values for each label are the same.

You also can write "doesn't contain," as AppleScript will expand the contraction when it compiles the script.

EXAMPLE | This script puts true into the result window:

"The Tao of AppleScript" **does not contain** "Zen"

SEE ALSO | *contains, is contained by, is not contained by, starts with, ends with*

## ends with

WHAT IT DOES | Determines if a string or a list ends with a certain value

SYNTAX | *list1|string1* ends with *list2|string2*

RESULT | Returns true if a list, or string, ends with the certain value.

NOTES | To determine if a list, but not a string, ends with another value, you must specify the entire item. For instance, the list {"The","Tao","of","AppleScript"} does not end with "ipt" since "ipt" isn't an entire item in the list. However, the above list *does* end with {"AppleScript"}.

EXAMPLE

This script puts true into the result window:

---

"The Tao of AppleScript" **ends with** "Script"

---

SEE ALSO

*starts with, contains, does not contain, is contained by, is not contained by*

## error

WHAT IT DOES

Exits a subroutine, returning an error to the main script.

SYNTAX

error *errorText* [number *errorCode*] [from *objectReference*]

RESULT

The main script receives an error where the error message is defined by the text in *errorText*. You can assign a code number to the error with an integer value for *errorCode*. You also can tell the main script which object generated this error by using the "from *objectReference*" optional parameter.

NOTES

If this subroutine is called from within a try statement, the error from the subroutine will cause AppleScript to execute the commands under the "on error" portion of the statement.

EXAMPLE

This script executes a subroutine that returns an error saying that an error has occurred and that its error code number is 1.

---

```
makeError()
on makeError()
    error "An error has occurred" number 1
end makeError
```

---

## exit repeat

| | |
|---|---|
| WHAT IT DOES | Exits a repeat loop from within the repeat loop. |
| SYNTAX | exit repeat |
| RESULT | Goes to the command immediately following the "end repeat" portion of a repeat loop. |
| EXAMPLE | This script beeps when x is equal to 3: |

```
copy 0 to x
repeat
    copy x + 1 to x
    if x is 3 then exit repeat
end repeat
beep
```

## get

| | |
|---|---|
| WHAT IT DOES | Gets information, either from another application or from AppleScript. |
| SYNTAX | get *expression\objectOrProperty* |
| RESULT | Returns the requested information. |
| NOTES | To use this command with other applications, those applications must support the "get data" Apple Event and the Object Model. |
| EXAMPLE | This script puts the first word in the first window in Scriptable Text Editor into the result window: |

```
get word 1 of window 1 of application "Scriptable Text
Editor"
```

| | |
|---|---|
| SEE ALSO | *copy, set* |

## if

WHAT IT DOES    Enables you to execute commands only if certain conditions are true.

SYNTAX    if *boolean* then *command*

if *boolean* then

    *commands*

[else if *boolean* [then]

    *commands*]

[else

    *commands*]

end if

RESULT    With the "if" statement, you can cause certain commands to run only under certain conditions. The commands within the conditional are only run if the Boolean in the conditional is true.

If you've included an "else" statement, those commands are run if the initial *boolean* is false. Optionally, you can place a conditional on an "else" statement, so that the commands under it will only run if the initial *boolean* is false, and the conditional attached to the "else" returns true.

NOTES    Any expression that represents a Boolean can be placed in *boolean*. For instance, you can write "if true then beep" and it will beep, because the boolean evaluates to true.

Once AppleScript has executed the commands under a conditional statement, it immediately moves to the commands following "end if." Thus, if the initial boolean is true, AppleScript never looks at "else" statements in that script.

EXAMPLE    This script first sets the variable x to 3, and then beeps because the expression "x=3" evaluates to true:

---

**copy** 3 **to** x

**if** x = 3 **then** beep

---

## ignoring

WHAT IT DOES    Allows ignoring of certain attributes when comparing two strings.

SYNTAX    ignoring *attribute1*[, *attribute2* ,..., and *attribute5*] [but considering *attribute1*[,*attribute2*,..., and *attribute5*]]

      *commands*

end ignoring

RESULT    When ignoring an attribute, AppleScript does not take that attribute into account when comparing the two strings.

NOTES    Possible attributes are shown in the table in the "Considering and Ignoring" section of Chapter 2, "Scripting Basics."

EXAMPLE    The following script puts true into the result window, because, when ignoring the white space in the two strings, "TheTao" is in "The Tao of AppleScript":

---

**ignoring** white space

    "TheTao" **is contained by** "The Tao of AppleScript"

**end ignoring**

---

SEE ALSO    *considering*

## info for

WHAT IT DOES    Returns assorted pieces of data about a particular file or folder.

SYNTAX    info for *filePath*

RESULT    Returns an information record about the file or folder specified by *filepath*. The "creation date" item is the date, in AppleScript date format, on the file or folder that was created. The "modification date" item is the last date, in AppleScript date format, on the file or folder that was last modified. The "locked" item is a Boolean that is true if the file/folder is locked, and false if it is not. The "folder" item is a Boolean specifying whether the *filepath* points to a folder or a file. If it's false, the file path specifies a file and AppleScript returns additional information about the file. The "file creator" item is the four-letter code for the application that created the file. The "file type" item is the four-letter string that indicates the type of the file. The "size" item is the size of the file in bytes. The "short version" item is a string that contains the short version string of the file. The "long version" item is a string that contains the long version string of the file.

NOTES    *filePath* must be a string that points to a file. This is in the format "Disk:Folder:...:Folder:File" and must be referred to as a file so AppleScript knows to interpret the string. This is done by placing the word "file" before the actual path to the file.

This command comes from a scripting addition named "File Commands."

EXAMPLE    This script gets info for the Finder on a hard drive named "Thendara" and places the record of information into the result window:

---

info for file "Thendara:System Folder:Finder"

---

SEE ALSO    *choose file, path to, list folder*

## is contained by

WHAT IT DOES    Determines if one value is contained within another.

SYNTAX    *string1\list1\record1* is contained by *string2\list2\record2*

RESULT    Returns true if the first item is contained within the second string; returns false if it is not.

NOTES    When comparing lists, a list is contained within another list only if all the items in the first list are contained in the second in the same order.

When comparing records, one record is contained within another if all the labels are the same and the values for each label are the same.

EXAMPLE    This script puts true into the result window:

---

"Tao" **is contained by** "The Tao of AppleScript"

---

SEE ALSO    *is not contained by, does not contain, contains*

## is not contained by

WHAT IT DOES    Determines if one value is not contained within another.

SYNTAX    *string1\|list1\|record1* is not contained by *string2\|list2\|record2*

RESULT    Returns true if the first item is not contained within the second string; returns false if it is not.

NOTES    When comparing lists, a list is contained within another list only if all the items in the first list are contained in the second, in the same order.

When comparing records, one record is contained within another if all the labels are the same and the values for each label are the same.

You also can write "isn't contained by", as AppleScript will expand the contraction when compiling the script.

EXAMPLE    This script puts true into the result window:

---

"Zen" **is not contained by** "The Tao of AppleScript"

---

SEE ALSO    *is contained by, does not contain, contains*

## list disks

| | |
|---|---|
| WHAT IT DOES | Gets a list of all the mounted volumes. |
| SYNTAX | list disks |
| RESULT | Returns a list where each item is a string that is the name of a volume mounted on your Desktop. |
| NOTES | This command comes from a scripting addition named "File Commands." |
| EXAMPLE | This script puts a list of all the mounted volumes into the result window: |

```
list disks
```

| | |
|---|---|
| SEE ALSO | *info for, path to* |

## list folder

| | |
|---|---|
| WHAT IT DOES | Gets a list of all the items in a folder. |
| SYNTAX | list folder *filePath* |
| RESULT | Returns a list of all the items in *filePath*, where each item in the list is a string representing the name of that item. |
| | Generates an error if *filePath* is not a folder or disk. |
| NOTES | filePath must be a string that points to a folder. This is in the format "Disk:Folder:...:Folder:" (note the final colon). AppleScript must be told to interpret this string as a path to an item on the desktop by using the word "file" before the string. |
| | This command comes from a scripting addition named "File Commands." |
| EXAMPLE | The following script puts a list of all the items in the System Folder on a hard drive named "Thendara" into the result window: |

---

list folder file "Thendara:System Folder:"

---

SEE ALSO    *info for, path to*

## load script

WHAT IT DOES    Loads all the script objects in a file into memory so that they can be used from a script.

SYNTAX    load script *filePath*

RESULT    The files specified by *filePath* are loaded into memory so they can be accessed as script objects.

NOTES    *filePath* must be a string that points to a file. This is in the format "Disk:Folder:...:Folder:File" and must be referred to as a file so that AppleScript knows to interpret the string. This is done by placing the word "file" before the path to the file.

This command comes from a scripting addition called "Load Script."

This script loads all the scripts in a file named "stringLib" in a "Scripting Libraries" folder on a hard drive named "Thendara" and places ""«script»"" in the result window to indicate that the scripts have been loaded into memory:

---

load script file "Thendara:Scripting Libraries:stringLib"

---

SEE ALSO    *run script, store script*

## mod

WHAT IT DOES    Divides two numbers and returns the remainder.

SYNTAX    *number1* mod *number2*

RESULT    Returns the remainder of the quotient of *number1* divided by *number2*

NOTES     When used in a mathematical expression with other operators, mod is executed at the same time as other division.

This operation always returns an integer number.

This operator is particularly useful when determining if one number is divisible by another. For instance, if you want to know if a particular number is even, you can find out if that number mod 2 is zero. If it is, then the number is even because there is no remainder when dividing an even number by two.

EXAMPLE     This script puts 1 into the result window:

---

**5 mod** 3

---

SEE ALSO     *div, ÷, \*, -, +, ^*

## offset

WHAT IT DOES     Finds out where one string begins within another string.

SYNTAX     offset of *subString* in *containerString*

RESULT     Returns an integer that tells you how many characters into *containerString subString* begins. If the command returns 0, *subString* was not found in *containerString*.

NOTES     *subString* must be written exactly as it appears in *containerString*.

This command comes from a scripting addition named "String Commands."

EXAMPLE     This script puts the number 5 into the result window, because "Tao" starts on the fifth letter of "The Tao of AppleScript":

---

offset of "Tao" in "The Tao of AppleScript"

---

SEE ALSO     *contains, is contained by*

## or

WHAT IT DOES     Determines if either of two Boolean values is true.

SYNTAX     *boolean1* or *boolean2*

RESULT     Returns true if either *boolean1* or *boolean2* is true; returns false if both are false.

NOTES     *boolean1* and *boolean2* can be any AppleScript expression that produces a Boolean value, such as "x = 4" or "true."

Each Boolean must be placed in parentheses.

If AppleScript sees that the first Boolean is true, it won't check the second Boolean.

EXAMPLE     This script puts true into the result window because the second expression returns a Boolean value of true:

```
copy 4 to x
(x = 3) or (true)
```

SEE ALSO     *and, not*

## not

WHAT IT DOES     Determines the opposite of a Boolean value

SYNTAX     not *boolean*

RESULT     Returns true if *boolean* is false; returns false if *boolean* is true.

NOTES     *boolean* can be any AppleScript expression that produces a Boolean value, such as "x = 4" or "true."

You must place the Boolean in parentheses.

EXAMPLE     This script puts true into the result window because the expression (x=3) is false:

> **copy** 4 **to** x
>
> **not** (x = 3)

SEE ALSO    *and, or*

## path to

WHAT IT DOES    Gets the pathname of any one of several special folders, the startup disk, or the frontmost application.

SYNTAX    path to [*specialFolder*|startup disk|frontmost application] [as *classType*]

RESULT    Returns the full path to the special folder you specify. *specialFolder* can be "Apple Menu Items" (or "Apple Menu"), "Control Panels," "Desktop," "Extensions," "Preferences," "PrintMonitor Documents," "Trash," "Startup Items," "System Folder," or "Temporary Items." You also may write "startup disk" or "frontmost application" to get the paths to those items.

The result can be coerced to a different type (such as a string) by using the optional "as *classType*" parameter, where *classType* represents the name of the class you wish to coerce the path to.

NOTES    This command comes from a scripting addition named "File Commands."

EXAMPLE    This script puts the path of the Apple Menu Items folder into the result window:

> path to "Apple Menu Items"

SEE ALSO    *info for, load script, run script, store script*

## random number

WHAT IT DOES    Generates a random number.

SYNTAX  random number [*number*] [from *lowestNumber* to
*highestNumber*] [with seed *number*]

RESULT  With no parameters, this command generates a random
decimal number between 0 and 1. If you place a single
number after the command, it will generate a random
integer between 1 and the number you typed. By using the
"from *lowestNumber* to *highestNumber*" parameter, this
command will return a random integer between the two
numbers you specify. You also can give this command an
initial seed value for the random number.

NOTES  Computers cannot generate truly random numbers, so
they must use "pseudorandom numbers." This means that
while you cannot predict the value of the number, it's not
truly random. To generate pseudorandom numbers,
computers use "seed" values and run them through a
complex mathematical equation. The result differs depending on the particular seed value. Usually, computers
use sources such as the number of ticks (sixtieths of a
second) since the computer was turned on, or the number
of seconds passed in the current day. These sources provide numbers that change constantly, and thus produce a
"random" number when put through the mathematical
equation.

You can specify a seed for this operation. The numbers
generated from a given seed will always follow the same
sequence of values, although each will seem random the
first time that seed is used.

This command comes from a scripting addition named
"Numerics."

EXAMPLE  This script generates a random integer between 1 and 100
and places that number into the result window:

---

```
random number 100
```

---

## repeat

WHAT IT DOES  Performs a set of commands repetitively.

SYNTAX  repeat

  *commands*

end repeat

repeat *integer* [times]

  *commands*

end repeat

repeat while *boolean*

  *commands*

end repeat

repeat until *boolean*

  commands

end repeat

repeat with *variableName* from *integer* to *integer* [by *integer*]

  *commands*

end repeat

repeat with *variableName* in *list*

  *commands*

end repeat

RESULT  With the first form of this statement shown above, the commands are run indefinitely. You must use the "Stop" button in Script Editor to terminate the script.

With the second form, commands run the number of times specified in *integer*.

The next two forms use Boolean values to determine when to stop.

The fifth form repeats the commands over an interval of numbers, with each number being placed into a variable. The number of times that the loop increments the variable each time is 1, but that can be altered with the "by" option.

The last form runs the commands in the repeat loop once for every item in the list, setting the variable to the current value in the list.

NOTES    By using the repeat with *variableName* from *number* to *number* and the "by" modifier, you can count from number to number. Using a negative number with the "by" modifier tells AppleScript to count backward. If you wanted the loop to count from 100 to 1, you may type the following:

---

repeat with i from 100 to 1 by -1

---

EXAMPLE    This script beeps and increments the variable x until x is equal to 3:

---

```
copy 0 to x
repeat until x = 3
    beep
    copy x + 1 to x
end repeat
```

---

## round

WHAT IT DOES    Rounds a decimal number to an integer.

SYNTAX    round *number* [rounding up|down|toward zero|to nearest]

RESULT    Without the optional parameter indicating how to round, this command rounds *number* to the closest integer. The "rounding *direction*" parameter enables you to tell AppleScript to round the number up (3.1 and 3.6 become 4), down (3.1 and 3.6 become 3), towards zero or to the nearest integer.

NOTES    When rounding a number where the decimal portion is .5, the command defaults to rounding up, if the number to the left of the decimal is odd, down if it is even.

Rounding a number to the nearest integer is no different than rounding with no parameters. However, this enables you to illustrate what is happening more clearly.

This command comes from a scripting addition named "Numerics."

EXAMPLE    This script rounds 6.47 up and places the number 7 into the result window:

---

round 6.47 rounding up

---

SEE ALSO    ÷, *div*

## run

WHAT IT DOES    Starts an application or runs a script object.

SYNTAX    run *appName\scriptObjectName*

tell application *appName* to run

tell *scriptObjectName* to run

RESULT    This command produces two different results. If it is sent to an application, it will start that application as if you had double-clicked on it in the Finder. If it is sent to a script object, it will run any commands contained directly in the script object (ignoring any subroutines within the object unless they are called directly within the object).

NOTES    Using run on an application works only if that application supports the four required AppleEvents. If the application you name doesn't, AppleScript will give you an error telling you that the application doesn't support AppleEvents. However, most applications support these events.

For techno-weenies, this command sends an "oapp" event to the application. This means that, upon receiving this command, an application will act as if it just started up, making new windows or any other actions, such as running scripts, that would happen at startup.

EXAMPLE

This script will run Scriptable Text Editor, or will result in it acting as if had just been started, if it's already running:

---

run application "Scriptable Text Editor"

---

SEE ALSO

*tell, activate*

## run script

WHAT IT DOES

This command runs a script from a file, or from a set of commands contained in a string, or in the language of another scripting component.

SYNTAX

run script *scriptFile\string* [with parameters *parameterList*] [in *scriptingLanguage*]

RESULT

When you specify a file with this command, it runs a script in a "run" subroutine. You can set up a string that contains several commands, separated by returns, and run that as if it were a script. By using the "with parameters *parameterList*" parameter, you can pass a set of parameters to the script, with each item in the list being a parameter to the script. If you are using another scripting language that is part of the Open Scripting Architecture, you can use the "in *scriptingLanguage*" parameter to specify which scripting component you wish to use for the script.

Any results of that script are returned back to the main script.

NOTES

When you point to a file with this command, you must point to it with a string in the format "Disk:Folder:Folder:File", using as many folders as are necessary to describe the location of the file. Furthermore, you must tell AppleScript to interpret this as a file description.

This command is stored in a scripting addition named "Run Script."

EXAMPLE This script runs a script that is stored in a file named "Tester" in a folder named "Scripts" folder on a hard drive named "Thendara" and puts the result of that script into the result window:

```
run script "Thendara:Scripts:Tester"
```

SEE ALSO *load script, store script*

## set

WHAT IT DOES  Sets the value of an object or variable.

SYNTAX  set *objectPath\variableName* to *expression*

RESULT  When this command is used, it sets the object or variable you specified with *objectPath/variableName* to the value you specified in *expression*.

NOTES  "Set" can be used to do "data sharing."

```
set y to {3, 4, 5}
set x to y
set item 1 of y to 6
x
```

The result of this script is {6,4,5}. A link is established between the two variables. When y changed, x changed.

When working with large lists or records, you can set up this kind of link between the two variables. This can help avoid problems due to memory limitations.

In order to use this command to control an application, that application must support the Object Model and the "set data" Apple event.

EXAMPLE    The following script sets the contents of the first window of Scriptable Text Editor to "The Tao of AppleScript":

**set the** contents **of** window 1 **of** application "Scriptable Text Editor" **to** "The Tao of AppleScript"

SEE ALSO    *copy, get*

## starts with

WHAT IT DOES    Determines if a string or a list begins with a certain value.

SYNTAX    *list1\string1* starts with *list2\string2*

RESULT    Returns true if the first item begins with the second value.

NOTES    To determine if a list ends with another value, you must specify the entire
item. For instance, the list {"The","Tao","of","AppleScript"} does not start with "Th" since "Th" isn't an entire item in the list. However, the above list does start with {"The"}.

You can also write "begins with" as a synonym for "starts with."

EXAMPLE    This script puts true into the result window:

"The Tao of AppleScript" **starts with** "The Tao"

SEE ALSO    *ends with, contains, does not contain, is contained by, is not contained by*

## store script

WHAT IT DOES    Saves a script object into a script file.

SYNTAX    store script *scriptObjectName* in *fileName* [saving yes\no\ask]

| | |
|---|---|
| RESULT | This command stores the script object you specify with *scriptObjectName* into the file you name in *fileName*. |
| | By using the optional "saving" parameter, you can tell AppleScript to save that script file, to not save it, or to ask (as it normally would) the user with a directory dialog box. |
| NOTES | To refer to a file with AppleScript, use a string that gives the *path* to that file. This string is in the format "Disk:Folder:Folder:File." To tell AppleScript that this is a file, you must precede it with the word "file." |
| | This command is stored in a scripting addition named "Store Script." |
| EXAMPLE | This script stores the script object *scriptObject* into a file named "Generic Libraries" in a folder named "Libraries" on a hard drive named "Thendara": |

```
store script scriptObject in file "Thendara:Libraries:Generic
Libraries"
```

| | |
|---|---|
| SEE ALSO | *load script, run script, choose file* |

## tell

| | |
|---|---|
| WHAT IT DOES | Enables you to address a particular application or other object. |
| SYNTAX | tell *objectPath* to *command* |
| | tell *objectPath* |
| | *commands* |
| | end tell |
| RESULT | By using the first form of the command, you can direct one command to an application or script object. With the second form, you can send several commands to one object. In addition, this second form sets up a default object path. If you don't specify the complete path to an |

object, AppleScript will finish it with whatever is in *objectPath*.

NOTES The first form of this command is useful if you wish to send a command to an application while talking to another application.

The second form of this command is useful when you have several commands to send to one application, or you wish to set up a shortcut for typing long object paths.

Using the "tell" command forces AppleScript to get all the information from an application about the commands it knows, and the information it can handle. If you have problems getting a command to run, try enclosing it in a tell statement that points to the application.

EXAMPLE This script uses the "tell" statement to set up a default object path to the first window of Scriptable Text Editor:

---

**tell** window 1 **of** application "Scriptable Text Editor"
    **get** word 1
**end tell**

---

## try

WHAT IT DOES Tries a set of commands. If an error is generated, the script will run an alternate set of commands, giving information about the error if desired.

SYNTAX try

    *commands*

> on error [*errorMessageVariable*] [number
> *errorNumberVariable*]
>
> *commands*
>
> end try

RESULT AppleScript first runs the commands within the "try" portion of this statement. If an error occurs, AppleScript runs the commands under "on error" by using the *errorMessageVariable* parameter. You can place the text of the error message into a variable to use it in your script. You can also use the "number *errorNumberVariable*" parameter to place the number of the error into a variable you define.

NOTES Using this command enables you to respond to errors from within your script, rather than having the script simply stop. This will make sure a script can continue when a problem occurs. It also gives more meaningful information to the user.

EXAMPLE This script tries to coerce a string into a number. It displays a dialog that tells you what went wrong if it fails, using a variable named "errorText" to contain the text of the error message.

---

```
try
    copy "The Tao of AppleScript" as number to
    wrongCommand
on error errorText
    display dialog "An error has occurred:" & errorText
end try
```

---

## with timeout

WHAT IT DOES Tells AppleScript to time out from receiving a reply from an Apple Event sent to another application.

SYNTAX    with timeout [of] *integer* second[s]

    *commands*

end [timeout]

RESULT    If AppleScript does not receive a reply from the target application in the specified number of seconds, it will continue with the next command. The "end" portion of this statement tells AppleScript which commands to apply the "with timeout" statement to.

EXAMPLE   This script will time out from the command sent to Scriptable Text Editor after one second:

---

**with timeout of** 1 **second**

 **set the** contents **of** window 1 **of** application "Scriptable Text Editor" **to** "The Tao of AppleScript"

**end timeout**

---

# Variables

AppleScript has a number of built-in variables that you can use in your scripts. This section describes them in detail.

## it

WHAT IT STANDS FOR    This variable can stand for two different things. When the script is in a tell statement, "it" contains the object path you put after the "tell" command. When used in a filter to extract data, "it" represents the object you're testing.

EXAMPLES    Using "it" in a "tell" statement:

---

**tell** window 1 **of** application "Scriptable Text Editor"

 **set the** contents **of it to** "The Tao of AppleScript"

 **get** word 1 **of it**

---

**end tell**

Here, "it" represents the first window of Scriptable Text Editor. Although this may seem pointless, since the scripts could function without the "it," using this variable makes more sense syntactically in one-line "tell" statements, as in the following:

**tell** window 1 **of** application "Scriptable Text Editor" **to get the** name **of it**

If you wish to find every occurance of the word "The" in a window in Scriptable Text Editor, however, you *must* use the "it" variable:

**get every** word **of** window 1 **of** application "Scriptable Text Editor" **where it is** "The"

Here, "it" refers to the word objects themselves.

## me

WHAT IT STANDS FOR    Refers to the current script object.

EXAMPLES    If you are within a script or script object, you can refer to it within the script itself by using me.

```
script sampleScript
    on add(x, y)
        return x + y
    end add
    on subtract(x, y)
        tell me to add(x, -y)
    end subtract
end script
```

In the above script object, one command is "add" and the other "subtract." Subtract uses the add command that is within the script object. To do so, it uses the phrase "tell me to add (x,-y)." This is a shortcut to enable you to work with other commands you've defined within the script object.

If you have established properties for your script object, you can use "me" to work with those properties. The following example illustrates this:

```
script sampleScript
    property name : "Derrick"
    on add(x, y)
        return x + y
    end add
    on subtract(x, y)
        tell me to add(x, -y)
    end subtract
    get the name of me
    get my name
end script
```

In this script object, there is a property called "name." If you want to use that property from within the script, you can ask for "the name of me" or "my name."

## pi

WHAT IT STANDS FOR   This variable stands for the number pi. Since pi is an infinitely long number, AppleScript uses 3.1415926535898 as an approximation.

EXAMPLES   You can make a script that will calculate the area of a circle, given a radius:

```
on areaCircle(radius)
    return pi * (radius * radius)
end areaCircle
```

## result

WHAT IT STANDS FOR   This variable stands for the result returned from a command. This variable is reset after each command. If a command does not return any information, "result" is empty.

EXAMPLES   This script displays the result from three commands in dialogs. This is a useful technique for debugging scripts, since it enables you to see the result at each point of the script:

```
3 + 3
display dialog (result as string)
get every word of window 1 of application "Scriptable Text Editor"
display dialog (result as string)
set x to 3
display dialog (result as string)
```

## return

WHAT IT STANDS FOR   This variable is used to represent the "return" character.

EXAMPLE   This script puts three paragraphs into Scriptable Text Editor:

```
tell window 1 of application "Scriptable Text Editor"
    repeat with i from 1 to 3
        set the contents to (the contents & "Paragraph " & i as string) & return
    end repeat
end tell
```

The "return" variable ensures each paragraph is really a paragraph by placing a return character after each one.

## space

WHAT IT STANDS FOR  This variable represents the space character.

EXAMPLES  This variable can be used to separate several words that may not otherwise have spaces in them, as in the following example:

```
copy "Derrick" to firstName
copy "Schneider" to lastName
display dialog firstName & space & lastName
```

## tab

WHAT IT STANDS FOR  This variable represents a tab character.

EXAMPLE  This script will make two columns of numbers in Scriptable Text Editor, with the column separated by a tab:

```
repeat with i from 1 to 5 by 2
    tell window 1 of application "Scriptable Text Editor"
        set the contents to the contents & i & tab & i + 1 &
        return
    end tell
end repeat
```

# The Tao of AppleScript

**'aete' resource**   A resource contained within a program describing the dictionary for that program.

**alias**   A keyword found in AppleScript indicating that the string to follow is a reference to a file.

**AppleScript**   Apple's system-level scripting language. It's designed to enable you to automate and connect different applications quickly and easily. For complete instructions, read the book.

**AppleScript Formatting** A menu command in Script Editor that enables you to change the way AppleScript formats compiled text. For more information, see Chapter 1.

**AppleScript-aware**   Refers to an application that can be controlled by AppleScript.

**applet**   The common term for a script application that does not support drag-and-drop.

**Apple event**   A system-level message sent from one application to another. The message instructs the receiving application to perform an action or return requested information to the sending application. These messages form much of the foundation on which AppleScript works. For more information, see Appendix 1.

**application**   A self-contained program that performs a set of related tasks and may allow you to create documents.

**application menu**   The menu in the upper right corner of the System 7 Macintosh screen. Pulling down this menu displays a list of all open applications. The menu appears as an icon in the menu bar—this icon represents the foreground application.

**attachable**   Refers to an application that enables scripts to be attached to elements of the user interface. For instance, choosing a menu command or pressing a button can run an AppleScript script.

**BMUG**   Berkeley Macintosh User Group. The coolest user group in existence. With more than 12,000 members in over 50 countries, this is also the largest Macintosh user group in the world. For more information, see "About BMUG" in this book.

**Boolean**   A type of data that can be either true or false. Usually the result of comparing two pieces of information by some criteria. For more information, see Chapter 2.

**bounds**   A set of numbers describing the size of a window. This set is a list of integers where the first item is the distance in pixels from the left edge of the screen to the left edge of the window; the second item is the distance, including the height of the title bar, from the top of the screen to the top of the window; the third item is the distance from the left edge of the screen to the right edge of the window; the last item is the distance from the top of the screen to the bottom of the window.

**bubble sort**   A method of sorting which compares pairs of items in a list—placing each pair in a specified order. Repeating the action over the entire list causes one value to move through the list and be placed at its proper position. A sorted list is produced by repeating the entire process within a script.

**bug**   A problem with a script that causes it to work incorrectly or stop with an error.

**class**   The category describing an object, such as "word" or "window." Also the category of an Apple event, such as "core" for core events or "aevt" for required events. For more information, see the first appendix.

**client application**   A program sending an Apple event.

**coercion**   Forcing AppleScript to interpret one type of data as another type of data. This is necessary for some commands and operations which only understand one type of data. For more information, see Chapter 2.

**command**  An instruction that performs a particular action. Some commands are built into AppleScript while others must be sent to applications or scripting additions for execution. For more information, see Chapter 2.

**comment**  A "note" in a script. A comment is not executed, but provides information about the script to a person reading it. For more information, see Chapter 4.

**commenting out**  The act of turning portions of script into comments, thereby preventing them from executing. This technique is commonly used when tracking down problems in a script. Lines can be commented out and then put back in until the line or lines causing the problem is found.

**compile**  The act of formatting the text and checking the syntax of a script. Uncompiled scripts are compiled automatically when they are run. For more information, see the description of what happens

when you click the "Check Syntax" button in Chapter 1.

**component**  Anything that uses the Component Manager to become a part of the System—enabling applications to take advantage of it.

**Component Manager**  A portion of the Macintosh System software that allows components to become active within the System—allowing applications to utilize them. Components differ from extensions in that extensions intercept calls to the System whereas components allow new calls to be made. This enables new functionality to be added to the System without releasing a new version of the software. The Component Manager is built in to System 7.1, but is also incorporated into the QuickTime extension.

**compress**  The act of removing redundant data from a file. Compressed files must be uncompressed before the data within the file can be used. Programs such as StuffIt Lite, included on the disk, compress files to reduce the space needed on the hard drive.

**concatenating** The act of making two or more pieces of data into one by appending one onto the end of the other. For more information, see Text, Lists, and Records in Chapter 2.

**conditional** A script statement that executes commands only if certain conditions are met. For more information, see Chapter 2.

**container object** An object which contains the object of interest. For more information, see "Objects" in Chapter 2.

**coordinates** A set of two numbers representing a position on the screen. Coordinates are written as a pair of integers where the first number is the distance from the left edge of the screen and the second number is the distance from the top edge of the screen to the position. For more information, see Chapter 3.

**core events** Those Apple events which developers are strongly encouraged to support in their applications and which represent the most likely ways to work with the data in that application. Some of the events in this group are Get Data, Set Data, Create, Delete, and Count.

**counting variable** A variable used in a repeat loop to track the number of iterations a loop has repeated or the current value in a list when traversing that list. For more information, see "Counting Repeat Loops" and "Traversing a List" in Chapter 2.

**creator** A four-letter code which represents the application with which a file is associated.

**custom events** The Apple events which a developer includes to deal with aspects unique to their application.

**date format** A string of characters representing a date and time in AppleScript format. Such a string must be preceded by the word "date" and enclosed in quotes, as in: date "Thursday, June 10, 1993 3:04:36 PM".

**declaring a variable** The act of assigning a value to a variable for the first time. Declarations tell AppleScript to prepare the variable for later use in the script. For more information, see "Variables" in Chapter 2.

**dictionary** Information about the commands and objects an application understands. This information is stored in the application or scripting addition in an "aete" resource. For more information, see Chapter 10 and Appendix 1.

**directory traversal**   The act of going through all the files and folders on a hard drive. A directory traversal typically starts at the top level of the drive, performing a given action on all the files and/or folders in that level. It then looks into each folder on that level, repeating the same. A directory traversal can perform the traversal on a specified folder.

**drag-and-drop**   A term describing the process of dragging an icon or icons onto the application icon until it highlights. During drag-and-drop, the files are not moved, but the application is run and acts on those files in a specified manner.

**droplet**   The common term for a script application that supports drag-and-drop.

**element**   An object or piece of information contained in an object; a subset of a larger group.

**error**   A message that is returned to the script when a command or application cannot be executed for some reason. The message contains a description of that reason.

**error checking**   The process of anticipating every possible user action, including potential mistakes and all possible responses to a dialog. Error checking prevents unpredictable results in response to unpredictable user actions.

**every**   A term used by AppleScript to specify all items of a given type of an object. The items are returned as a list. For more information, see the "Commands" section in Chapter 2.

**execute**   The act of running or performing a script or command.

**expression**   One or more constants and/or variables, possibly joined by an operator, representing a single value. Anything from the number 3 to "word 1 of window 3 of application 'Scriptable Text Editor'" is an expression.

**Extensions folder**   A folder within the System 7 System Folder where extensions are kept. Scripting additions cannot be used by AppleScript unless they are in a folder named Scripting Additions in the Extensions folder when the Macintosh is started.

**file reference**   A reference which points specifically to a file or folder. It is preceded by the word "file" and the string that follows it contains the name of the hard drive, followed by the names of the folders and finally the file, each separated from the others by a colon character. For example: file "Internal:Sounds:derrick laugh".

**file sharing**   A feature of System 7 which allows Macintoshes on a network to exchange files.

**flag**   A variable which represents a given condition, usually of type Boolean. The variable is set to a particular value early in the script. That value is later checked to determine if certain commands should be run. For more information, see "Variables" in Chapter 2.

**flow of information**   The path of information as it moves among different programs and/ or people.

**formatting**   The act of modifying text—usually the style and/or size—to improve legibility. It typically includes indentation within conditionals, loops, subroutines, tell statements, and script objects. For example, Script Editor will change the text of all key words in a script to bold-face text.

**functional-area events**   Those Apple events intended to perform a specific type of function. For instance, an Apple event that manipulates text.

**global variable**   A variable whose value can be accessed and changed by subroutines, as well as the main script. For more information, see "Making it Better" in Chapter 4.

**icon**   A pictorial representation of a file, button, or piece of information.

**ID number**   A number unique to a specific resource of a given type in a given file.

**if...then statement**   Synonym for "conditional" statement.

**increment**   The specified discrete amount that a value increases when it is contained within a loop.

**integer**  A number which does not have a decimal component.

**invisible file**  A file which is not visible from the Finder. Some programs may allow you to see them if you select files with the directory dialog box.

**keyword**  In Apple events, a four-letter code that tells the server application how to interpret the attached data.

**label**  A user-defined keyword that names an item of an AppleScript record; parameter of a subroutine's "given" statement.

**library**  A collection of scripts kept as a source for frequently-used routines.

**list**  A type of data that contains several pieces of unlabeled data. For more information, see the "Variable" heading in Chapter 2.

**local variable**  A variable whose value is accessible only by the subroutine in which it is declared. Other subroutines that use a variable of the same name will not alter the variable declared in first subroutine.

**macro utility**  A program which records user actions for play-back at a later time.

**message**  In AppleScript, a command which the script receives, either from the System or from the script itself. When the command is received, AppleScript runs a subroutine of the same name as the message. For more info, see Chapter 7.

**modifier**  A keyword that alters the result of a command. For instance, the "not" modifier reverses the result of a comparison. For more information, see the "Conditional" header in Chapter 2.

**network**  Two or more computers linked electronically for the purpose of sharing resources.

**Object Model**  A hierarchichal structure defined by Apple for selecting information within an application. Each object may contain and be contained within other objects. Objects are distinguishable by unique properties. For more information, see Chapter 2.

**object path**  A description of an object's position that includes all of its contents, and how the object is differentiated from similar objects. For more information, see Chapter 2.

**objects**   The items in an application that hold information; elements of an application addressable by AppleScript. For more information, see Chapter 2.

**Open Dictionary...**   A menu command in Script Editor that enables an application or scripting addition to access the dictionary.

**operation**   Symbols or keywords which manipulate data in some way, such as the use of mathematic symbols to manipulate numbers.

**optional parameter**   A portion of a command not necessary for the command's execution. When supplied, it provides more specific information to the command or alters the its behavior. For more information, see Chapter 2.

**orders of precedence**   A series of rules describing the order in which mathematical operations are performed. For more information, see "Variables" in Chapter 2.

**parameter**   A supplemental phrase or word providing information to a command. For more information, see "Commands" in Chapter 2.

**pixel**   A single point on the screen. Short for "picture element."

**pop-up menu**   A menu that is contained within a dialog or window, rather than in the menu bar. Usually represented by a rectangle with a drop shadow and a downward-pointing triangle. When the user presses on this rectangle, the menu is displayed at that position.

**position**   The location of an object, either on the screen or relative to other objects. For more information, see Chapter 3.

**program**   A set of commands that interacts with the System software. This includes stand-alone programs (applications and extensions) and programs which need to be loaded and run by another program, such as scripting additions.

**program (v.)**   To write a set of commands that perform some task.

**Program Linking**   The portion of file sharing software that enables programs to send Apple events to applications on the network.

**property** An attribute of an object. For more information, see "Objects" in Chapter 2.

**QuickTime** A system extension from Apple that allows video and picture compression for viewing on the Macintosh. Also provides the Component Manager to System 7 and System 7.0.1 so that AppleScript may be used.

**real number** A number which has a decimal component.

**record (n.)** A type of data which contains several pieces of labeled information. For more information, see "Variables" in Chapter 2.

**record (v.)** The act of composing scripts, reflecting the actions of the user, for later play-back. AppleScript can record a user's actions within recordable applications.

**recordable** Describes an application which allows AppleScript to record user actions within that application and compose a script reflecting those actions.

**reference** A description that points to an object or file. The reference is the path to that object or file.

**repeat loop** A structure which repeatedly executes a set of commands until a given condition is met. For more information, see Chapter 2.

**required events** Those Apple events which Apple requires for full System 7 compatability; specifically Open Application, Open Documents, Print Documents, and Quit.

**required parameter** A portion of a command necessary for the command's execution, providing information to the command or altering the command's behavior. For more information, see "Commands" in Chapter 2.

**reserved word** A word which has special meaning to AppleScript. This includes all the built-in commands and commands from the scripting additions, as well as words that are available to AppleScript while it is communicating with a specific program.

**resources** Collections of data which contain the elements of the Macintosh interface specific to an application or to the System itself. These collections may be modified by programmers and users to easily alter icons, menus, and other elements.

**run-only script**   A script that can only be executed and not edited. This is useful for hiding scripts so that others cannot view or modify them.

**save dialog box**   A dialog box that permits a file to be saved with a name you assign and in a folder you specify.

**script**   A set of commands that AppleScript understands and can execute; a file containing such commands.

**script application**   A script that can be executed just like an application; that is, by opening on its icon in the Finder.

**script editing area**   The portion of the Script Editor window in which scripts can be written and edited.

**Script Editor**   A simple application provided by Apple with the AppleScript package for writing and editing scripts.

**scriptable**   Describes an application that can be controlled via AppleScript. Implies that the application contains a dictionary.

**Scriptable Text Editor**   A simple text editor provided by Apple with the AppleScript package. It is designed as a model for AppleScript support in future applications. Scriptable Text Editor is fully scriptable and recordable.

**scripting**   The act of writing scripts.

**scripting addition**   A program that adds functionality to the AppleScript language, but is not a complete application. Scripting additions cannot be used by AppleScript unless they are in a folder named Scripting Additions in the Extensions folder when the Macintosh is started.

**Scripting Additions folder** A folder within the Extensions folder. Scripting additions cannot be used by AppleScript unless they are in the Scripting Additions folder when the Macintosh is started.

**scripting language**   A computer language that uses scripts to automate tasks.

**server application**   A program receiving an Apple event.

**Shareware**   Software which may be legally used at no

charge for a specified period of time; thereafter a fee must be paid to the author. Time periods and fees vary—refer to the software documentation.

**some**   A term used by AppleScript to specify any random item of a given type within an object. For more information, see the "Commands" section in Chapter 2.

**splash screen**   A window or picture that is displayed when a script or program is started. Usually displays credits or information about the program.

**stack**   The name for a document created with the HyperCard application.

**string**   A collection of characters.

**subroutine**   A set of commands set aside from the main portion of the script. Subroutines are run only when specifically addressed in the main script by a single command. In AppleScript, the name of that command is the name of the subroutine.

**syntax error**   A problem that is caused by an improperly-written script. When

AppleScript attempts to compile a script, it will fail if any syntax errors are detected.

**System**   A generic term for the Macintosh system software.

**System 7 sound file**   A file containing a digitally-sampled sound that System 7 will play when the file is opened in the Finder.

**System Folder**   A folder where all the files needed for the Macintosh System to run properly are kept.

**Taoism**   A Chinese philosophy and religion based on the teachings and writings of Lao-tzu. Emphasizes simplicity and appreciation of Nature and the world. For more information, read *The Tao of Pooh* and *The Te of Piglet* by Benjamin Hoff.

**temporary variable**   A variable which is used to hold a value for a short period of time—typically used to hold the value of another variable while it is being modified.

**text**   A type of data in AppleScript represented by characters enclosed in quotation marks. Also an object in Scriptable Text Editor. For more information, see "Variables" in Chapter 2.

**the result window**   A window in Script Editor that displays the information returned by a command. For more information, see Chapters 1 and 2.

**thru**   A phrase that specifies a range of objects, as in "words 1 thru 14." For more information, see Chapter 2.

**traversing**   In AppleScript, executing a set of commands once for each item in a group of objects.

**type (file)**   A four-letter code that represents the category of a file. For example, text files are of type "TEXT".

**uncompress**   To expand a compressed object so that it is restored to its original size. See compress.

**user error**   An error which occurs because the user of a script has done something wrong, usually entering a value that cannot be used.

**variable**   A container for information. When written in a script, AppleScript uses the value contained in the variable. For more information, see the "Variables" section in Chapter 2.

**variable star**   A star whose brightness varies because of internal changes or periodic eclipsing of mutually revolving stars.

**where**   A term in AppleScript that enables reference to any objects meeting certain criteria. Equivalent to "whose." For more information, see Chapter 2.

**whose**   A term in AppleScript that enables reference to any objects meeting certain criteria. Equivalent to "where." For more information, see Chapter 2.

**window 1**   A term in AppleScript for the frontmost window of an application.

**workaround**   A set of commands that achieve a particular result when there is no straightforward method for achieving that result . For more information, see Chapter 7.

**Zen**   A branch of Buddhism that focuses on meditation, self-contemplation, and intuition as the road to enlightenment. For more information, read *Zen and the Art of Motorcycle Maintenance*, by Robert Pirsig.

# BMUG

# A Computer Users Group

*BMUG is a membership-based non-profit organization dedicated to helping users of graphical interface computers. It represents the interests of over 12,000 Macintosh users in more than fifty countries.*

BMUG offers something for everyone. Here are a few of the reasons that more than 12,000 people belong to BMUG:

The BMUG Newsletter — Published twice a year, each Newsletter contains 400 pages of reviews, reference material, and commentary (but no advertising!).

Planet BMUG, the BMUG BBS — A FirstClass graphical interface electronic Bulletin Board Service. Use your modem to exchange messages with BMUG members around the world, send mail via the Internet, and download software from BMUG's vast software library.

The Helpline — Access to our technical Helpline is available to members during business hours by phone, fax, or in person.

The Software Library — One of the largest and most up-to-date collections of Publicly Distributable software anywhere. It is sold on disks and CD-ROM or can be downloaded from the BBS.

Publications and CD-ROMs — BMUG publishes CD-ROMs of Shareware, and books on electronic bulletin boards, scripting, and software programs.

The Meetings — BMUG holds weekly and monthly general meetings and Special Interest Group meetings virtually every night of the week. See interesting product demos, meet other computer users, and hear the latest industry rumors.

## Contacting BMUG

### By Phone

| | |
|---|---|
| Announcement Line | (510) 849-9114 |
| Business Office | (510) 549-2684 |
| Fax | (510) 849-9026 |
| Planet BMUG, the BMUG BBS | (510) 849-2684 |
| BMUG Boston BBS | (617) 721-5840 |
| BMUG—product orders only | (800) 776-BMUG |

### By Mail

BMUG Inc.
1442A Walnut Street, #62
Berkeley, CA  94709-1496

### Our office location

BMUG Inc.
2055 Center Street, cross street Shattuck Ave.
in downtown Berkeley

## The BMUG Philosophy

BMUG started as a small user group in 1984, shortly after the introduction of the Macintosh. As a non-profit corporation BMUG strives to give the plain, unbiased truths about product performance and the industry in general. We don't sell advertising in our newsletters and make it quite clear that we will not exchange good reviews for product donations. BMUG is neither affiliated with, nor receives monetary support from, Apple Computer or any other for-profit entity.

*Our goal is clearly stated in our motto:*
*"We're in the business of giving away information."*

# BMUG Memberships

BMUG is member-supported. Membership privileges include semi-annual issues of the famous BMUG Newsletter, technical assistance, and access to Planet BMUG, the BMUG BBS.

Join BMUG today and find out why MicroTimes lists BMUG among the 100 most important influences on the computer industry and said, "BMUG is what every user group dreams of becoming."

*California Business* magazine rates BMUG in the top 100 of California's Hottest Digital Information providers.

Select one of the following membership packages for individuals:

## Six Month Membership – $28

- One issue of The BMUG Newsletter
- Access to The BMUG Helpline for one person for six months
- A Six month account on The BMUG BBS (60 min/day)

## Contributing Membership – $45

- Two issues of The BMUG Newsletter
- Access to The BMUG Helpline for one person
- An account on The BMUG BBS (60 min/day)

## Sustaining Membership – $70

- Two issues of The BMUG Newsletter
- Access to The BMUG Helpline for one person

- An account on The BMUG BBS (90 min/day)
- Access to online magazines (such as BoardWatch, NewsBytes, USA Today)

## Hero Membership – $100

- First Class mailing of two issues of The BMUG Newsletter
- Access to The BMUG Helpline for one person
- An account on The BMUG BBS (90 min/day)
- Access to online magazines (such as BoardWatch, NewsBytes, USA Today)
- Acknowledgement in The BMUG Newsletter

## Satellite Club Membership – $250

- First Class mailing of two issues of The BMUG Newsletter
- Access to The BMUG Helpline for one person
- An account on The BMUG BBS (120 min/day)
- Access to online magazines (such as BoardWatch, NewsBytes, USA Today)
- Two of each BMUG product released during the year of your membership (except PD library floppy disks)
- Acknowledgement in The BMUG Newsletter

## The BMUG Newsletter

BMUG Newsletters are published twice a year. Each is approximately 400 pages long, contains no advertising, and is written and edited by BMUG members, volunteers, and staff. We encourage you to contribute your efforts as well. Remember, the only way to receive the current Newsletter is to be a BMUG member!

The Newsletter includes software and hardware reviews, "how-to" guides, commentaries on the computer industry, and Choice Products— BMUG's respected product recommendations.

Each Newsletter comes with a disk of the latest and greatest Shareware and Freeware, as well as a program to help you access our electronic Bulletin Board Service.

## BMUG Online

### Planet BMUG, the BMUG BBS

Got a modem? That's about all you'll need to get online with BMUG on our electronic Bulletin Board System (BBS). Members can request a free account on our FirstClass, graphical user interface BBS. We support baud rates from 300 to 14,440, on all 17 lines. Thousands of members log on and discuss every subject under the sun. We exchange mail with Internet via UUCP mail. Much of the most current Shareware and Freeware is available.

BMUG is also on many of the commercial forums across the nation. You can reach BMUG at the following electronic addresses:

| | |
|---|---|
| America Online: | BMUG or BMUG1 |
| AppleLink: | UG0001 |
| Internet: | bmug@aol.com |
| CompuServe: | 73237,501 |
| Prodigy: | HCHT96B |
| The WELL: | bmug |

## Technical Assistance

### The Helpline

BMUG's Helpline for members is the only place where you can get technical help on virtually any subject pertaining to the Macintosh. BMUG volunteers and staff answer our phones weekdays from 9:30 AM to 5:30 PM Pacific Time. We attempt to return your call within two business days. BMUG accepts technical questions via fax as well.

### Emergency Data Recovery

Broken hard drive? Crashed floppy? If you're a member we'll do our best to recover your data, for free. There are no guarantees, but we have many tools at our disposal and years of experience using them. An appointment is required so call our Helpline first. If you can't make it to us, we'll arrange for you to mail it in to us. You can save hundreds of dollars, and we'll even let you join *after* your hard drive crashes. BMUG does RAM upgrades for members as well.

## BMUG Software Library

BMUG has one of the largest collections of Freeware and Shareware software in the world. The library contains over four hundred 800K disks organized into categories such as Utilities, Fonts, Games, Education, etc. Disks are available to both members and non-members at $4 each, to cover our costs. Specially priced disk packs are available. BMUG carefully and painstakingly checks everything we sell for viruses.

*BMUG strongly encourages users to support Shareware authors and their efforts by sending in Shareware fees.*

## BMUG Publications

## The 1993 BMUG Shareware Disk Catalog

A 700+ page compendium of the disks which make up the BMUG Shareware Library, the largest and most complete Macintosh Shareware library in the world. You can get it cheapest from us, but look for it in stores, published by Addison-Wesley.

## BMUG's Quicker QuickTime

Learning about video from scratch can be harder than learning about your first computer. The authors of this book don't assume you are an expert in either, but by the time you read the last page, you will understand how computers and video can combine to make something very exciting happen. The book includes a disk including Apple's QuickTime, MoviePlayer, and QuickTime movies.

## Zen and The Art of Resource Editing-Third Edition

A series of articles to help you navigate through the cryptic world of ResEdit. The newest edition is 240 pages long and includes System 7 tips. The book comes with a disk containing the current version of ResEdit and templates.

## ToonWare—A Humor Interface

This collection of the humorous and the absurd is a sure bet for any computer enthusiast. Ninety-six pages of comic art—the perfect gift for anyone with a sense of humor and a Mac.

## BMUG CD-ROMs

## BMUG's TV-ROM™

An eclectic CD-ROM collection of QuickTime movies. Contains over 100 PICT files and nearly 400 MooV files of people, places, animals, and things.

## The BMUG PD-ROM™ version B

In addition to our entire library of Shareware and Freeware, the PD-ROM contains stuff available only from BMUG (such as News-letters back issues). With over 600M of fonts, games, and other programs, it's the best source of Publicly Distributable software and all System 7.1 compatible and 32-bit clean.

## The BMUG ResEdit Collection, CD-ROM

From the authors of Zen and the Art of Resource Editing, comes a collection of cool and exciting things! Includes the latest version of ResEdit, new editors, thousands of icons, patterns, resources, utilities, QuickTime, and Frontier Runtime.

## Other BMUG Products

## The BMUG Tie-Dyed T-Shirt

This t-shirt has become legendary. The fashion statement of BMUG.

## Tote Bag

Our 100% cotton all purpose tote-bag. Tested across the globe by BMUG staff and volunteers with great results.

## Meetings

All of BMUG meetings are open to the public. You do not have to be a member to attend. We welcome new and old Macintosh users alike. Call the BMUG Announcement line at (510) 849-9114 for times, dates, and locations.

### Main Meetings

BMUG holds weekly Macintosh meetings on the UC Berkeley campus. Approximately 100 to 150 members and non-members gather to discuss the latest industry gossip, ask technical questions, and watch vendors demonstrate new and soon to be released software and hardware. The meetings are free of charge, open to the public, and there is a raffle at the end of every one.

### BMUG•West

Each month BMUG holds a Macintosh meeting at the Exploratorium's McBean Theater in San Francisco from 6:00 PM to 9:00 PM on the last Monday of the month. Though they have the same format as our main meetings, including the raffle, they are smaller and more intimate.

### BMUG•South

A monthly meeting in San Jose. Every third Monday at the Santa Clara County United Way office at 1922 The Alameda, unless otherwise noted on the BMUG announcement line. The meeting starts at 6:30 PM.

### Special Interest Groups (SIGs)

BMUG has meetings almost every week night, and some on weekends as well, on specific fields of interest. All SIGs meet in our offices in Berkeley unless otherwise noted and are free of charge and open to the public.

# *Index*

# D

## P

## Q

## T

## X-Z

## W

# Included on the Tao Disk

**AppleScript:** The AppleScript package, straight from Apple! All you need to script your Macintosh—includes AppleScript, Script Editor, and Scriptable Text Editor.

**QuickTime:** View digital video on your desktop! Apple's QuickTime, for digital video viewing and picture compression. You'll need this if you are running System 7.0 or 7.0.1.

**Finder Liaison:** Control the Finder without lifting your mouse finger. This is an AppleScript-aware application which enables you to create, delete, move, or otherwise manipulate files, directly in the Finder.

**DialogRunner:** Make your own dialog boxes in your scripts! With this addition you can add a real interface to your own scripts.

**Progress Bar:** Add a progress bar to any script. With this AppleScript-aware application you'll never again be in the dark about progress on your Macintosh.

**ResMover:** Move sounds, rename fonts, install Fkeys—all with this scripting addition. You can play with the resources in any file.

**StuffIt Lite:** A fully scriptable, recordable, and powerful compression program. It's always been a great program, but it's incredible with AppleScript.

**Folder Watcher:** A control panel that can actually watch your desktop for you! Automate decompression of anything you put in a folder, or set off an alarm when someone drops something in your inbox folder!